MENTORING

The Ministry of
Spiritual Kinship

Edward C. Sellner

MENTORING
The Ministry of Spiritual Kinship

AVE MARIA PRESS
Notre Dame, Indiana 46556

Edward Sellner is an Associate Professor of Pastoral Theology and Spirituality at the College of St. Catherine in St. Paul, Minnesota, and has worked as a chemical dependency counselor and consultant, including five years with Hazelden in Minnesota. He holds his PhD from the University of Notre Dame and is the author of numerous journal articles on spirituality and recovery from chemical dependency. His books include *Christian Ministry and The Fifth Step*, and *The Fifth Step: A Guide to Reconciliation* (both from Hazelden/Harper & Row).

Many of the personal observations about C.S. Lewis quoted in Chapter 2 are excerpted from *C.S. Lewis at the Breakfast Table*, edited by James T. Como. Copyright © 1979 by Macmillan Publishing Company.

Excerpts from *The Golden String* by Bede Griffiths, copyright © 1980 by Templegate Publishers, Springfield, IL. All rights reserved. Used with permission of the publisher.

Excerpts from THE JERUSALEM BIBLE, copyright © 1966 by Darton, Longman & Todd, Ltd. and Doubleday & Company, Inc. Used by permission of the publisher.

Chapter 2, ''C.S. Lewis as Spiritual Mentor,'' originally appeared in shortened form in the October, 1987, issue of *The Way*, published at Heythrop College, London, England.

International Standard Book Number: 0-87793-426-6
0-87793-425-8 (pbk.)
Library of Congress Catalog Card Number: 89-81098

Cover design by Elizabeth J. French

Printed and bound in the United States of America.

For John and Mary, Ed and Elaine,
my first mentors,
and Joe and Fritz,
spiritual friends

Contents

Introduction

There is an emerging consensus in our society and church on the importance of people acting as mentors and guides to others. Developmental psychologists are affirming the contribution mentors can make regarding career and professional choices; self-help groups such as Alcoholics Anonymous and Alanon speak of the value of sponsors for ongoing recovery. In the area of Christian spirituality the need for sponsors in the conversion process and spiritual guides for ongoing adult transformation is once again being recognized as important, if not essential, to the life of faith. As a pastoral theologian and former chemical dependency counselor, I have been interested in these various forms of mentoring for some time. I believe that they can be of significant help not only for young people in their formative years, but for all of us throughout life as we face unexpected crises and so-called predictable transitions. I am also convinced that the ministry of spiritual mentor or guide was never an exclusively clerical domain, and that more lay people should consider this particular form of ministry.

This book is intended to help people name some of the mentoring they have already experienced or done, and also to help lay people in particular recognize their own potential as spiritual mentors.

Mentoring in its broadest sense is something any of us can do, and need to do, especially when we've entered mid-life. If Christian faith and values are consciously brought to others, this mentoring, I believe, becomes an important form of contemporary ministry.

Spiritual mentoring, one particular form of mentoring, may be characterized by greater depth and may be more explicitly concerned with our vocation and relationship with God, but as we will see, it cannot be totally removed from the more ordinary forms, since they are so closely intertwined. While spiritual mentoring may overlap with the profession of spiritual direction as it has developed in the Western Church, spiritual mentoring is an age-old

9

Christian tradition, a calling and a gift more common than perhaps previously thought. It depends more on mutuality, reciprocity and friendship than direction given from "the top down" or on a relationship with someone who supposedly has all the answers while the other is only a passive recipient of such wisdom. As a contemporary form of ministry, it is much needed.

Whether "ordinary" or "spiritual," however, mentoring in its most fundamental sense is about transformation, helping someone else encounter his or her deeper self, which Jung calls "the larger and greater personality maturing within."

Chapter 1 discusses some of the rich history of mentoring, from psychological and theological perspectives, in the context of spirituality and some of my own experiences with significant mentors.

Chapter 2 examines in depth one lay person's ministry of spiritual mentoring: Oxford professor and Christian apologist C. S. Lewis. Lewis is presented as an example of how spiritual mentoring can be an effective ministry for any one of us and how it can take a variety of forms.

Because an important aspect of contemporary spirituality is the recovery of lost traditions, Chapter 3 explores one of those traditions, the Irish *anamchara* or "soul friend," that has made a significant contribution to Christian spirituality. This tradition's creative origins can teach us a great deal about spiritual mentoring today.

Chapter 4 explores one specific area of spiritual mentoring, that of "vocation," and offers suggestions on how to continue to discern our own "call of life to the soul."

Chapter 5 examines how dream figures can act as mentors to us and shows how attention to dreams is a long and ancient Christian practice.

Chapter 6 discusses a mentor, especially a spiritual mentor today, as a pioneer, concerned with ageless realities of the soul and of a larger community than ourselves, a spiritual community that transcends space and time.

The Conclusion brings together the insights from our reflections, which can help guide us in our own ministries of mentoring.

As I suggest in this book, one important pattern in the ministry of mentoring is acknowledging that one has been mentored first. I would like to do so here. This book could not have been written without what psychologist Rollo May calls the "vivid experiences" that have left their mark on my life and thought: those many mentoring relationships that have made a difference in my life. In addition to the "long distance" mentoring of those such as Robert Kennedy, C. S. Lewis, Thomas Merton, Carl Jung, Henri Nouwen and Rosemary Haughton, some of my most significant mentors have been my teachers. I especially remember Joe Kelly, who taught me history and social studies at the College of St. Francis, Fort Wayne, Indiana, and who got me involved in the politics of 1968; from graduate school at the University of Notre Dame I am grateful to Tjaard Hommes, Don McNeill, Morton Kelsey, Jim and Evelyn Whitehead, John Gallen, Enda McDonagh and Ed Malloy.

I am also grateful in particular to two supervisors during a year of clinical pastoral education for their loving acceptance and patient guidance: Frank Garvey at Willmar State Hospital and Gordie Grimm at Hazelden Rehabilitation Center in Minnesota. They seemed to know me better than I knew myself. That year working with recovering alcoholics and their families changed my life, raising questions that continue to demand attention in my teaching and my research.

When I was 1986-88 national chair of the National Association for Lay Ministry (NALM), John Reid, Suzanne Elsesser, John F-X Burton, Marian Schwab, Zoila Diaz, Tim O'Connell and especially Dolores Leckey acted as friendly guides for me in my work on national and international levels to represent the concerns and experiences of lay ministers in the United States. I want to say thank you to them as well as to Christiane Brusselmans and Monsignor Peter Coughlan, who introduced many of us to Rome, the Vatican, and especially the Piazza Navona at the time of the Synod on the Laity in October 1987. I am grateful to Evelyn and Jim Whitehead, Emilie and Bill Griffin, Leonard and Helen Doohan, Joan Timmerman, A. M. Allchin, Benedicta Ward, Margaret Hebblethwaite and Walter Hooper for their support and specific suggestions in the art of writing a book. Special thanks also go to my colleagues and students at the College of St. Catherine, St. Paul, Minnesota, who consistently have pushed me, through their questions and encouragement, deeper into the vast, rich and diverse history of Judeo-Christian spirituality. I especially appreciate the critical comments and support of Suzie Hall, Mary Erickson, Kay Vandervort, Joyce McFarland, Mary Kay Medinger, Mark Scannell, Ken Schmitz, and the typing help of Kay Kirscht. My special thanks also go to Frank Cunningham, general manager and editor at Ave Maria Press, for his early encouragement and continuing critique. Needless to say, without the love of my wife, Jo Anne, and my two sons, John and Daniel, this book could not have been written.

Most of all, I am grateful for the first mentoring I received. This book is dedicated to my grandparents, John and Mary (Foy) Lipetzky, who cared for me on their farm when I was very young, and to my parents who continue to teach me about love, friendship and generativity. From my father, a tavern owner, I learned about the importance of hospitality and first heard about "lay confession" when he told me that he as a bartender probably heard more confessions than the parish priest. My mother taught me about compassion and that, as in the Eastern Orthodox tradition, the shedding of tears is not a sign of sentimentality but of great wisdom.

This book is also dedicated to two spiritual mentors whose help in discerning the direction of my life is inestimable: Joe Hennen, who was so intimately involved in my own form of adult conversion, and Fritz Pfotenhauer, my guide into the world of dreams and the unconscious when I was a graduate student at Notre Dame.

Finally, for the writing of this book I have drawn upon the wisdom of a spiritual community transcending my own time and culture, people whom I have never physically met, and yet who have affected my life and thought in many conscious and unconscious ways. Like the images in our dreams, this larger community reveals how much we are a part of one another when we communicate at a level that can only be described as a communion of souls. This meeting of souls can happen, according to the Anglican spiritual writer A. M. Allchin, through "the discovery of a saint, a book, an icon from some other part of the Christian world which suddenly we find to be intimately linked with us; the meeting with someone far away in space and time who yet becomes our friend and contemporary." However it happens, in the recognition of our mutuality bonds are made, community is formed and a deep inner sense of happiness pervades our lives despite the struggles and conflicts that persist. As the Old Testament wisdom figure Jesus, son of Sirach and author of the Book of Ecclesiasticus, writes: "Happy is the person who finds a friend, and the person who speaks to attentive ears" (Sir 25:9).

Although we have never met, one of my "long-distance" mentors has been the author and spiritual writer Frederick Buechner. In *The Sacred Journey*, he writes, "If God speaks anywhere, it is into our personal lives that he speaks." On my journey, my own sacred journey, God has spoken in my relationships with mentors and friends. As you reflect with me on the topic of mentoring, I hope that what is said will help you reflect on your sacred journey and perhaps help you identify the friends through whom God speaks.

ONE

A Form of Love

Mentoring is best understood as a form of love relationship.

Daniel Levinson, *The Seasons of a Man's Life*

The signs of the times clearly point to an increased interest in spirituality. Dedicated church members and members of religious communities have always acknowledged the importance of the spiritual life. Self-help groups such as Alcoholics Anonymous and Alanon have stressed for years the importance of spirituality for sobriety and ongoing recovery.

But now something more is happening, a revival of interest in spirituality and religion perhaps akin to the Great Awakenings that swept the United States in the 18th and 19th centuries. Groups ranging from New Age adherents to evangelicals and members of mainline denominations are discussing and reading about spirituality. Books like Scott Peck's *A Road Less Travelled* stay on the best-seller lists for months. New periodicals and ecumenical journals, such as *Weavings*, are being printed, and religious publishers tell of an ever-increasing demand for books on prayer. The great books written by the wisdom figures of the Judeo-Christian heritage enjoy renewed popularity as readers discover a wealth of insights helpful with present struggles.

Retreat houses and houses of prayer are sought out to escape busy schedules and find quiet solitude and spiritual guidance. Many of us are taking advantage of ministry and spirituality formation programs in parish and academic centers, which ultimately enrich not only the participants, but also the communities and work places to which we belong. Each year distant shrines, churches and holy places associated with our spiritual roots receive millions of visitors who, like the characters in Chaucer's *Canterbury Tales*, "long to go on pilgrimages." Journaling and the recording of dreams have become popular opportunities for spiritual growth.

This phenomenon is happening worldwide. Some of it has its dark side, manifest in the rise of fundamentalist cults and sects, and a brand of self-righteous conservatism, often limited in knowledge of the religious traditions themselves. It has its positive side as well.

Much of the increasing interest in spirituality may be a reaction to over-reliance on material goods for happiness. As Bill Moyers, an astute observer of the American scene, suggests:

> I think at the heart of so much restlessness of the day is a spiritual vacuum. There is a yearning for meaningful lives, a yearning for values we can commonly embrace. I hear an almost inaudible but pervasive discontent with the price we pay for our current materialism. And I hear a fluttering of hope that there might be more to life than bread and circuses.

Some of this turn toward interiority may be due to the aging of our population as we live longer, advancing well into mid-life and beyond. Perhaps much of it, as Robert Bellah asserts in *Habits of the Heart*, is related to the fierce competition and individualism that characterize so much of American life, and the consequent thirst for genuine community.

Whatever the causes of this phenomenon, I believe much of its origins lie in our yearning for more knowledge of our familial roots and spiritual heritage, our desire for some form of guidance in developing more meaningful lives, and ultimately in a restlessness of heart that only God can fulfill.

What is spirituality about? What are some resources that are available to us? A story may help clarify the meaning of the term and offer some insight on our being drawn to the divine.

Contemporary Spirituality and Mentoring

One day my younger son and I were alone in our home, an old Dutch colonial house with a lot of rooms upstairs and down. Daniel was 2 years old at the time, and as the afternoon progressed he wandered out of my sight. After not hearing any sounds for some time, I became suspicious—as any parent would—and went in search of him. I found him in my upstairs study playing quietly.

As I watched silently for a few moments unobserved, Daniel turned his attention from the toy fire truck he was holding to a tiny painted icon of Jesus located on a small table near the window. Without a moment's thought he suddenly leaned over and gave the icon a gentle kiss. Then, just as quickly, he returned to the fire truck and his play.

His simple act, done so spontaneously, took me by surprise. I knew that he had never seen me kiss the icon. I knew too that he was not fully aware of whose picture was portrayed there, or the rich history of spirituality it contained. And yet he had kissed the icon so naturally in the midst of what he enjoyed doing that I wondered what was behind his gesture of love and respect.

"Daniel," I said, interrupting his play, "who is that man whose picture you just kissed?" Without hesitating he replied, "He's a good guy, Dad, a good guy."

As a parent whose profession is theology, I was amazed at how my son had hit upon one of the essentials of our Christian tradition's understanding of faith and God. Oblivious to so much that can be related about Jesus, as well as to all the controversies over his identity which have divided Christians for centuries, Daniel had recognized the goodness, gentleness and wisdom of the man portrayed by the Eastern Orthodox artist so many years ago. He evidently saw in Jesus's face a person he could trust and love as a friend.

In some ways many of us today are like my son Daniel, not fully knowing who God is in all God's mystery. Yet on conscious and unconscious levels we are drawn to the reality of God through our human experiences of love and goodness.

This is what spirituality is about: being drawn to the sacred through the icons of our lives, that is, the images, symbols, rituals, experiences and, most important, the relationships that transform us by their love. It is about developing a relationship with God, the Holy One and source of goodness, who may seem very distant and unknowable at times, and yet is present to us as friend, often in unexpected ways and seemingly hopeless situations.

Spirituality in its broadest sense is, quite simply, a way of life that reveals an awareness of the sacred and a relationship with the Holy One in the midst of our human fragility, brokenness and limitations. It is about the way we live and interpret the world and the sacred mystery that surrounds us; the ways we celebrate important events such as birthdays, anniversaries, retirements and deaths in the lives of our families and friends; the ways we find support—and give it—in our conflicts and painful transitions.

Spirituality includes seeing our work as more than making a living (as important as that is); work becomes a genuine opportunity for service, a way of contributing to other people's lives. Spirituality is the responsibility we show our surroundings and our environment, the respect we have for our forests, mountains, rivers, lakes and seashores. It especially involves our attitude toward our everyday life, the way we spend our time. Are we merely wasting or killing time, or are we attempting to discover the sacred dimensions of life all around us?

In a basic sense spirituality is about the quality of our relationships, the ways we care for each other, including the ways we welcome those who are different from us into our lives and families. All the great spiritual traditions agree that spirituality encompasses all those dimensions of our lives that make us human; that is, not only prayer and worship, but our work, play, sexuality, gifts, talents and limitations too.

Spirituality is influenced for the Christian in a most significant way by the person and ministry of Jesus; the Sacred Scriptures, which tell his story; and the life of the ongoing community that bears his name. Through Jesus we have been given an awareness that our time on this earth is sacred, that we share a sacred journey, that our God has entered human history and taken on a human face. Christian spirituality includes the many ways throughout history that Christian individuals and communities have responded and continue to respond to the awareness of God's transforming love.

There are many ways of nurturing and strengthening our awareness of the sacred and our relationship with the Holy One. Some of these resources can be found in the customs and rituals of our churches. Our great communal celebrations, especially the Eucharist, and our hearing the gospel proclaimed and homilies preached can be opportunities for personal change and spiritual growth. Our parishes, as places of renewal, may provide us with workshops, retreats and small groups where we can come together for prayer, reflection and support.

Another resource of tremendous value is a friend or group of friends, a sponsor, a mentor, a spiritual director. These people can help us clarify the questions of our lives. Through their presence and compassion, we can discover options, make choices and ultimately fulfill the unique calling that is ours. Whether lay or ordained, spiritual mentors can become facilitators of spiritual growth and inner healing.

Experiences of Being Mentored

Each of us can recall a time when we wanted someone to talk with, to listen to our concerns, to help us discover or clarify a barely perceived direction in which we needed to go.

When we are young and searching for identity and meaning, we look outward to others, sometimes to heroes or heroines, surrounded by stories and deeds and myths. These people bring out the ideals and convictions stirring within us, and as mentors, teachers and guides introduce us to aspects of ourselves of which we were unaware. For me, the turbulence of the '60s and the lives and deaths of two men stand out as significant.

While John Kennedy made me proud of my Irish ancestry and my Roman Catholicism, and invited me to ask how I could best contribute to the lives of others, his younger brother Robert taught me about the importance of dreams and acting upon them. After the president's sudden death I decided to major in history and social studies in college. I began to follow Robert Kennedy's career with increasing interest and growing hope. When Bobby held a child in his arms, a child of poverty, he made me aware of a part of the nation I had not known; when he spoke to students in South Africa and South America, he brought those lands to my attention for the first time; when he broke bread with Cesar Chavez, he taught me about the injustice toward migrant workers; when he questioned the direction the war in Vietnam was taking, he confirmed my own fears and doubts. In the summer of 1967 I decided to act on my emerging convictions. I spent those hot, humid months in black neighborhoods in New Orleans; there, I received much more from the young people and their parents than I was able to give. In the fall of that year I helped form the Young Democrats' Club at college and was elected its first president. At the same time I was preparing to spend the following summer in Bogota among the South American poor.

Bobby Kennedy inspired me, as he did many others. His words, like those of his older brother, were filled with vivid images that elicited from listeners the desire to respond in some way. His own intimate relationship with suffering also gave him credibility. He told a group of students in South Africa on a visit there in 1966:

> Each time a man stands up for an ideal, or acts to improve the lot of others, or strikes out against injustice, he sends forth a tiny ripple of hope, and crossing each other from a million different centers of energy and daring, those ripples build a current that can sweep down the mightiest walls of oppression.

I had reflected upon those words, and as the war continued, as the predictions of a light at the end of the tunnel were constantly contradicted by the daily headlines, as the antipoverty efforts became lost in a bottomless well, I hoped he would announce his candidacy. When he did it was still winter, with snow in the air, and a small group of us began gathering the thousands of signatures needed to get his name on the ballot in Indiana, the first primary state he was to enter in his presidential race.

Bobby flew into Indianapolis on a warm spring evening in March to officially place his name on the Indiana ballot. My friends and I were part of a crowd outside the old courthouse—our anticipation and restlessness increasing as time seemed to slow and then come to a halt. Around me, seated on a wall overlooking the courthouse steps, were many other students, small children with their parents, people young and old, black and brown and white, well-dressed and poorly clad. In the doorway, blocked off by a rope, stood a woman with two green carnations held tightly in her hands. All of us talked and joked and sang as we waited, and then at last we heard police sirens in the distance, announcing the candidate's approach.

Stepping out of the darkness into the glare of television lights, Bobby Kennedy made his way to the front as the mood of the crowd suddenly changed from quiet whispering to cheering and screaming, pushing each other to get close enough to touch him or shake his hand. Women threw their arms around him or tugged at his sleeves; young fathers held their children above their shoulders so they could see; television cameramen and lights were shoved about. As he climbed the courthouse steps, I reached down from where I had been waiting and shook his hand. He went on, stopped and picked up a megaphone, and then began to speak above the din. He spoke briefly that night about changing America and bringing the presidency back to the people, and about his determination to fight against all odds, for the war was continuing to escalate, the poor were still being ignored, and the divisions in the country were growing deeper each day. Then he put the megaphone down, and the crowd surged forward once again, carried on by its own excitement and enthusiasm. I noticed, as Bobby reached the roped-off area where the woman with the carnations stood, that she had nothing to present to him but two broken, twisted stems. Her flowers had been crushed by the surging, pushing crowd.

When Bobby Kennedy died, so soon after the death of his older brother and Martin Luther King, my world of dreams and idealism and confidence in changing America was shattered. I left for South America a few days after his burial, overcome by a sense of desolation, going through the motions of being alive. As I worked with the poor in Colombia that summer and reflected with other college students about our program and our faith, I wanted to shout out to anyone who would listen or could possibly understand: "No! There is no God; there is no hope of change. We are alone!" I remained silent, allowing the currents of darkness to churn within, wearing an outer mask that hid so much—even from myself. When I returned to the United States in August, I flew to Washington, D.C., and went directly to the graves at Arlington. Silence lingered in the humid air—a tremendous silence compared to the noisy, excited, singing crowds in the hopeful spring that year. I stood there, filled with anger and resentment and despair, unable to accept the absurdity and madness that had brought these leaders to this grassy knoll.

For sometime afterwards I continued to live without hope. Given much, I was grateful for little; surrounded by a culture, religion and heritage of beliefs, I affirmed nothing as my own; living in a situation of freedom, I felt only chaos and confusion within. I was blind, in darkness, stumbling day by day in a world that I had not created and felt apathetic about. I had sought peace within my own country and a small Asian land by working in Robert Kennedy's presidential campaign and had seen it end in a hotel hallway. I had spent my summers in the crowded black ghettoes of New Orleans and the stinking hovels of Bogota, Colombia, wanting to have an effect—*some* effect—on eliminating poverty and hunger from the lives of those people who had touched my life. Instead, I discovered within myself a war, a poverty of spirit, a hunger for direction. I wanted freedom and yet was unaware of its awfulness and awe-fullness.

Two years later, during a year of clinical training while working with recovering alcoholics, I came to the realization that, like them, I needed to acknowledge and reconcile all the disparate feelings and experiences of my life. Feeling powerless not only from my grief over Bobby Kennedy's death and my own loss of faith, but from all those unresolved issues about intimacy, sexuality and vocation that concern a young adult, I reached out to a person who was there when I needed someone or something—I didn't know what. Joe listened to my history, my story, said yes when I had been hearing only no, and accepted my fears, despair, loneliness and inner darkness.

A flame flickered in the night, and it seemed that suddenly there was a God, a Someone greater than any one of us, a Being who moves as a consuming fire or gentle breeze or a rushing wave in the lives of individuals and nations throughout the history of humankind. For the first time all the religion classes I had attended and all the theology books I had read began to make some sense. There was a Reality that went beyond words, and the words and thoughts of others before me became a real part of my inner dialogue.

In retrospect, my experience with Joe was a holy experience, one that revealed to me a God who had always been so close and yet so far away, a God not only of the head, but of the heart. It was a turning point; it was a ''Yes, I believe''; it was the beginning of a way out of the darkness of a cave. Most surprising of all, this event of self-disclosure with a friend became an encounter not only with a loving God, but with my deeper self, an encounter, as Augustine says so well in the *Confessions*, ''forcing me to look in my own face.''

That event with a friend one evening so long ago became identified in my mind with the title of an Eugene O'Neill play, but rather than a long day's journey into night, it was for me a long night's journey into day. The tears of grief, guilt, confusion and remorse I shed during that evening made room for the healing presence of God, and when I awoke the next morning, I experienced a joy and sense of freedom I had never felt before.

When I decided to speak with Joe, an older man who was both a counselor and teacher, I did not know that that would happen; nor did I have a specific word—other than *friend*—to describe our relationship. Only later did I discover the name. Joe was a mentor and in many ways a spiritual guide. He became what another theologian, Rosemary Haughton, calls an "agent of transformation" in my life. While Robert Kennedy had mentored me from afar, introducing me to the Christian values of compassion and social justice, and the ongoing need to change our society and church in light of them, it was Joe's care, compassion and attentive listening that introduced me to the living reality of God. Because of both men's mentoring, the direction of my life changed.

Mentoring Today

Perhaps the mentors, teachers or guides who come to your mind are very different from those I just described. Perhaps they appeared for you at other times of your life, without the significance I have attached to mine. Perhaps you would not describe them in such a dramatic way, equating them, as I do, with a hero or a conversion experience. Possibly you would. However our experiences and perceptions differ, we all have had people who affected us in a positive way, calling us beyond ourselves. If we did not recognize their importance immediately, often hindsight provides an appreciation of their value and significance.

Before we explore some of our Judeo-Christian traditions as they relate to the ministry of being a spiritual mentor, we may come to a better appreciation of mentoring by briefly examining the origins of the term and some contemporary understandings of it.

The concept of mentoring is by no means a recent phenomenon. The word itself, simply defined by the Oxford American Dictionary as "a trusted adviser," finds its origins in ancient Greece. In the *Odyssey*, Mentor is the name of the trusted friend who in Ulysses' absence protects, nurtures, educates and guides his son Telemachus into adulthood. What is interesting about this mythic figure is that Mentor is described as an old man, a shepherd of the people, and often impersonated by the goddess Athene. On one occasion, we find, for example:

Now to these men came the daughter of Zeus, Athene, lik-
ening herself in voice and appearance to Mentor. Ulysses
was happy when he saw her, and hailed her saying,
"Mentor, help me from hurt, and remember me, your
companion and friend, who have done you much good. We
two grew up together."

In the works of developmental psychologists contemporary
mentoring is also associated with the roles of nurturing, educating
and guiding. Daniel Levinson, a Yale psychology professor, says
that the basic mentoring relationship is simply friendship with
someone a little more experienced, a person who acts as a guide in
regard to a new career, profession, job or developmental stage.
"Ordinarily," Levinson states, a mentor is "several years older,
a person of greater experience and seniority in the world." Levinson goes on to warn us that the relationship itself should not be
defined strictly in terms of formal roles but in terms of the character of the relationship and the functions it serves.

Those functions may include acting as a *teacher*, someone
who enhances a person's skills and intellectual development; a
sponsor, who may use his or her influence for the other's entry and
advancement; a *host* and *guide*, who welcomes the initiate into a
new occupational and social world, and acquaints him or her with
its values, customs, resources and cast of characters; an *exemplar*,
whom the protege can admire and seek to emulate; a *counselor*,
who provides counsel and moral support in times of stress; and
most important, according to Levinson, a *facilitator of the other
person's dream*, the vision of self and the life he or she wants to
lead as an adult, the vocation or call that so many are attempting to
clarify for themselves today in society and church. Levinson acknowledges the complexity of the mentoring relationship and describes it as a transitional relationship, one that can end with
strong conflict, hurt, resentment and bitter feelings. One recalls
the split that took place, for example, between Freud and Jung, or
F. Scott Fitzgerald and Hemingway, or between Jesus and the disciple who betrayed him with a kiss. There are often complex reasons for such a seemingly destructive termination, but it may be
simply that each has outgrown the other and is threatened by the

lack of what was once a profound resonance between them. Levinson says that ultimately we must see mentoring as a form of love relationship, one that is not easily turned on or off. Paradoxically, sometimes only after the separation between mentor and protege does the inexperienced person absorb more fully the admired qualities of the mentor. One's personality is enriched as the mentor figure becomes a more intrinsic part of oneself and, Levinson adds, ''the internalization of significant figures (like mentors) is a major source of development in adulthood.''

Levinson and other developmental psychologists affirm the need for mentors at all stages of life, especially during childhood, adolescence, young adulthood—and even into mid-life. Another recognized authority in the field of developmental psychology, Erik Erikson, delineates the stages of what he calls ''psychosocial development'' and describes the need for not only individuals, but also institutions to provide caring relationships. Such relationships allow the infant to learn trust; the child to attain autonomy, initiative and a sense of industry; the adolescent to achieve personal identity; and the young adult to experience what intimacy is all about.

While many psychologists agree with Erikson's basic presuppositions, there is more discussion today of the importance of mentoring for young adults beyond their intimacy needs. Perhaps because of increased anxiety over the job market and competition between men and women over those limited jobs, mentoring is now associated with the ability to make career choices and gain competence in one's field.

In *Seasons: Women's Search for Self Through Life's Stages*, Anita Spencer describes one of the major tasks of the season of spring, age 17-28, as the forming of mentor relationships. It is important, she says, to find someone who can help the young woman explore the adult world, make important choices regarding work, marriage and family, and form an adult identity. Female mentors are scarce, Spencer believes, especially in the world of work, because ''the few women who might serve as mentors are often too beset by the stresses of survival to provide good mentoring.'' Male mentors, she adds, are just as scarce.

Linda Phillips-Jones in *Mentors and Proteges*, dramatically claims that "finding and making use of the right mentor is the most critical step you'll ever take in your career." She also notes that mentors "can significantly help you reach your major life goals."

Career guidance and making choices are not the only advantages of having mentors. Self-help groups such as Alcoholics Anonymous and Alanon have recognized the value of sponsors for ongoing recovery for over 50 years; and, as my own life story shows, in the area of religious conversions, mentors can be a great help. Jim and Evelyn Whitehead remind us that as a form of love relationship mentoring offers a model of adult intimacy that is "nonsexual." (I would prefer that they used the word *non-genital*, since all our relationships are colored and influenced by our sexuality. Not to acknowledge that can often lead to a great deal of confusion, guilt, mixed signals and even genital acting out. We cannot evade the sexual component to our relationships, *especially* those characterized by any degree of intimacy.)

Thus we see an emerging consensus about the importance of mentoring for people in their formation years. I would add from my own experience as coordinator of a pastoral ministry program at a Catholic women's college that we need mentors in our later years too. Ask those many men and women changing careers or professions, or those women entering the job market for the first time or re-entering the academic environment for a degree or certificate.

It is also becoming apparent that adults, especially in mid-life, need *to act as mentors* for others in relationships that manifest, according to Erikson, generative care. From my own story I am beginning to see that just as I needed mentoring in my young adulthood years, so also mentors such as Robert Kennedy and my friend Joe had to become mentors in order to live up to their own calls to political and spiritual leadership.

The Stage Called Mid-life

Most psychologists agree that mid-life begins in our 30s or early 40s and continues into our early 60s. Jung describes the time between 35 and 40 as the beginning of significant change in the human psyche, a change that brings with it many difficulties if we are unprepared or uninformed. "We cannot live the afternoon of life according to the program of life's morning," he says.

Jung also tells us that "there is something sunlike within us, and to speak of the morning and spring, of the evening and autumn is not mere sentimental jargon." Describing the various seasons of life in *Modern Man in Search of a Soul*, he warns that "the afternoon must have a significance of its own and cannot be merely a pitiful appendage."

Whatever images one uses to describe mid-life, it is experienced in different ways by different people. Gender may make a difference, at least at this point in our cultural development. George Vaillant, for example, says that at age 40—give or take as much a decade—"men leave the compulsive, unreflective busy work of their preoccupational apprenticeship, and once more become explorers of the world within." Marjorie Lowenthal and her research colleagues found that women in their mid-years, although also experiencing a movement toward interiority, often experience a need to refocus their generative energies to the world outside of home and family. Many women, of course, have already done so by that age, especially as more choose career and family life during their young adulthood years.

Both sexes experience a need to feel and be recognized as competent. They also experience what Carol Bly in *Letters From the Country* calls "a sense of time left," a perception that the days on our calendars are numbered. With a discernment of our mortality comes a special urgency. Bly insightfully describes how this can have its advantages. In Madison, Minnesota, "a lost Swede town" of two thousand people, 45-year-old women finally start dropping out of "idle social intercourse" over coffee twice a day and "choose to topple into their inner lives instead." She also tells how a constantly cheerful minister in town, recovering from a critical illness, preached for an entire winter the first serious, thoughtful sermons of his life. While a number of people complained that his sermons had gone morbid and negative, Bly believed that they hadn't. "He simply had learned a sense of *time left*," which according to Bly, gets us all to ask the right questions.

One of those questions, whether a person is male or female, single or married, a parent or not, is *Can I, will I, be responsible for nurturing life?* This challenge in mid-life, Erikson tells us, is a conflict between generativity and self-absorption, and he defines the former as "primarily the concern for establishing and guiding the next generation."

Becoming generative includes a willingness to use our knowledge and influence responsibly in service that goes beyond ourselves. Mid-life and this challenge of generativity mark a critical time in an adult's life, a turning-point in personality development. To ignore the challenge, to become self-absorbed and narcissistic will only lead to greater immaturity, a stifling of creative and nurturing energies, and ultimately the greater possibility of experiencing old age with less integrity and greater despair.

Psychologists warn us that in mid-life we also need to acknowledge and reconcile four polarities within us if we are to have the capacity for greater generative care: young/old, destruction/creation, masculine/feminine, attachment/separateness.

We experience ourselves in mid-life with a new awareness that we are both young *and* old, in-between, as it were, and certainly closer to death itself. We experience a strong urge to create *as well as* a capacity to destroy, and we often feel guilty about the hurtful things that we have done or said to parents, wife, husband, children, friends and even rivals. We discover the need to accept both the yin and yang of our personalities. Men, traditionally more aggressive, may need to become more nurturing; women, often more people-oriented and self-effacing, may need to become more assertive.

Finally, we have a special need for togetherness and solitude, as Anne Morrow Lindbergh counsels in *A Gift From the Sea*. These polarities exist within each of us, so it is not that we should attempt to eliminate either, but rather move toward a new integration of both. Levinson says that, although these polarities are not specific to mid-life, they operate during those years with special force.

Overall, the development of maturity in any of us is the responsibility of all. Maturation is a communal process, in which all ages need encouragement, friendship and guidance. Older members of the human family must contribute to the process as mentors if they are to experience any sense of well-being, happiness and personal enrichment. Jung says that while older people in primitive tribes were almost always recognized as the guardians of the mysteries and customs, our modern culture seems to have set that aside. His words confront us: "Where is the wisdom of our old people—where are their precious secrets and visions? For the most part our old people try to compete with the young."

Psychologists remind us that to be human is to care. Whether we are young or old or somewhere in between, we need to be cared for as well as to care for others. The rich Judeo-Christian tradition tells us that to care is God-like; that, as Paul says, to minister to others is "to imitate God, as children of his that he loves" (Eph 5:1). That tradition also reminds us that we will be judged—or in more subtle ways we will judge ourselves—on the quality of care we have shown.

Our Judeo-Christian Heritage: A Caring God

The quality of our care and caring relationships are intimately related to spirituality and mentoring. When we turn to the Judeo-Christian spiritual heritage, we find that this theme is as old and young as the People of God. From the beginning of time, we are told, God called us into being, made in God's image, male and female (Gn 1:27), given a world and life that is fundamentally good. Before our loss of innocence, we lived in a beautiful garden and walked with God as mentor and friend (Gn 1:26-31). Despite our acts of violence and willful separation, during our times of despair when we wonder if there is any God at all, the stories of the Old Testament continuously remind us that God cares for us beyond our wildest expectations. These stories, psalms and poetry reveal God manifest in diverse ways and forms. There is, for example, God as a feminine wisdom figure, who "in each generation passes into holy souls" making them "friends of God and prophets." "She makes all things new" (Wis 7:27). As counselor, she offers "comfort in cares and sorrow," and "when life is shared with her there is no pain," only gladness and joy (Wis 8:9-

16). Knowing and understanding everything, she acts as a teacher and guide (Wis 9:10-11).

This caring and wise God is also portrayed as a servant figure who is worthy of emulation in his self-emptying: "Ours were the sufferings he bore, ours the sorrow he carried. . . . On him lies a punishment that brings us peace, and through his wounds we are healed" (Is 53:4-5). God is the source of a prophet's call, a vocation that includes both comforting and challenging God's people. Isaiah's understanding of his call is one that another would later identify with: "He has sent me to bring good news to the poor, to bind up hearts that are broken; to proclaim liberty to captives, freedom to those in prison, . . . to comfort all those who mourn" (Is 61:1-3).

This theme of the caring God as friend, wisdom figure, counselor, guide, teacher, servant, wounded healer, liberator, comforter, heart-binder and bringer of good news becomes incarnate in human history. Jesus, this special Son of God, teaches all sons and daughters of God about God's care and their own responsibility for offering care to other sisters and brothers. At the beginning of his public ministry Jesus quotes his mentor, Isaiah, and he himself becomes recognized as teacher, mentor, rabbi (Lk 4:18-19). He reminds his proteges that we are the salt of the earth and the light of the world (Mt 5:13-16) *if* we serve through a ministry of friendship with one another. As mentor, he shares with us what his life experiences and his God have taught him:

> I call you friends,
> because I have made known to you
> everything I have learned from my Father.
> . . . I commissioned you
> to go out and to bear fruit,
> fruit that will last; . . .
> What I command you
> is to love one another (Jn 15:15-17).

In another part of the gospel stories Jesus tells us: "It is enough for the disciple that he should grow to be like his teacher" (Mt 10:24-25). Advising compassion, that we "not judge, and you

will not be judged'' (Mt 7:1), he also advocates trust: "I am telling
you not to worry about your life and what you are to eat, nor about
your body and how you are to clothe it'' (Mt 6:25). Finally, he
describes with a dramatic story the criterion by which we will be
judged:

> Then the King will say to those on his right hand, "Come,
> you whom my Father has blessed, take for your heritage the
> kingdom prepared for you since the foundation of the
> world. For I was hungry and you gave me food; I was
> thirsty and you gave me drink; I was a stranger and you
> made me welcome; naked and you clothed me; . . . I tell
> you solemnly, in so far as you did this to one of the least of
> these brothers [and sisters] of mine, you did it to me (Mt
> 25:34-40).

The history of Christianity reveals how well we have sometimes lived up to his vision of a loving and just kingdom, and how
often we have failed to do so. Within that history there are many
examples of gifted people who helped others grow in holiness and
wisdom.

The Spiritual Mentor in the Christian Tradition

The rich tradition of spiritual mentoring in Christianity clearly
transcends differences in personality, sex, age and culture.

From the desert tradition we are given Antony and Pachomius, pioneers in Christian asceticism, who remind us that spirituality demands discipline. From Ireland the Christian shaman Columcille tells us that sometimes we may feel like exiles in our
search for God. Twelfth-century English Cistercian Aelred of
Rievaulx counsels us on the joys of spiritual friendship, and the
14th-century mystic Julian of Norwich assures us that all will be
well. From Germany Meister Eckhart speaks of creation and the
awe fundamental to Christian living. From Greece Gregory Pala-
mas teaches us to pray continuously from the heart. From Italy
come the two Catherines, of Genoa and Siena; the first describes
the immense love of God, and the second reminds us that even
church authorities may need to be challenged to accept ongoing
reform. From Spain Ignatius guides us in the discernment of spir-

its, and Teresa and John give us directions in interior castles and dark nights of the soul.

Wise pastors of the Protestant tradition such as Luther, Zwingli and Calvin speak of the priesthood of all believers, the need for ministry to include all sorts of people, lay and ordained, women and men, single and married. Bunyan, Fox and Wesley remind us that grace abounds and life is a pilgrimage, that we need to pay more attention to the inner light, that confession is good for the soul. And in more recent times the Anglican converts Evelyn Underhill and C. S. Lewis share with us mystics and myths, adult stories for children and children's stories for adults, while Thomas Merton and Dorothy Day confront us with the need to relate prayer and social justice.

In many ways their writings follow the predictable pattern found in the Jewish Talmud where age 30 is described as a time for attaining full strength, 40 for understanding, and 50 for giving counsel. The people in the Christian tradition reveal even more; adult conversion or a profound religious experience led many of them in their 20s or early 30s to a ministry of mentoring in mid-life and later years, sometimes even giving counsel much earlier than the 50 years mentioned by the Talmud. Augustine, for example, was in his early 30s when he was converted—with the help of two mentors, the bishop Ambrose and Monica, his mother. He went on to found his own community of friends, become a bishop and write the *Confessions*. Julian of Norwich writes that when she ''was thirty years and a half,'' she received the illness she had requested as well as the famous ''shewings,'' which became the basis for her theology of Jesus as mother and her ministry as spiritual guide. Merton was baptized at the age of 23 and went on to become a college teacher, a mentor to novices in his Trappist community, a spiritual director of his own abbot and, through his writings, a guide to millions of other people. C. S. Lewis was 31 when he ''admitted that God was God, and knelt and prayed'' in his room at Oxford. He spent the rest of his life ministering as teacher, guide and mentor in the classroom and outside of it. Jesus himself, after a profound affirmation in the waters of the Jordan and time spent alone in the desert, began a public ministry that included a great deal of mentoring at the age of 30. That ministry, so ordinary in many of its dimensions, and profoundly spiritual at the same time, continues in the lives of those who call themselves Christian today.

Age and experience can make a difference, and for many midlife can result in a flowering of creative talent, compassionate care and shared wisdom. Other patterns also emerge when we consider the broad scope of our heritage.

One important pattern is that the ministry of mentoring often begins with the experience of being mentored. The story of the Egyptian desert *abba* Antony is fairly typical. We are told by his biographer, Athanasius, that after an adult conversion one of the first things Antony did was go to a neighboring village and find "an old man who had practiced from his youth the solitary life." According to Athanasius, "when Antony saw him he emulated his goodness." This old man was only the first of many mentors for Antony, for "he observed the graciousness of one, the eagerness for prayers in another; he took careful note of one's freedom from anger, and the human concern of another—getting attributes of each in himself, and striving to manifest in himself what was best from all." Years later, after struggling with the demon in the desert, Antony becomes a spiritual mentor to many others, and, "before long, by the attraction of his speech, a great many monasteries came into being, and like a father he guided them all." He told the monks, "I, as your elder, will share what I know and the fruits of my experience."

A second pattern is that mentoring in the form of spiritual guidance is not limited to only "spiritual" affairs, God, and prayer—it includes all of life. Commenting on the correspondence of John Henry Newman, for example, editor Joyce Sugg writes in *A Packet of Letters* that "the largest group [of letters] and the most interesting is concerned with spiritual advice." In those letters Newman does offer words of comfort and guidance, but he also discusses a cat falling from a church ceiling narrowly missing his head, how children can be a source of companionship, and even about "waiting for a London dinner, thinking six would be a probable time for a lawyer, but he does not come till seven."

A third pattern is that mentoring does not have to end so sadly or bitterly as Levinson predicts. The mentoring relationship can be transformed into a relationship characterized by the mutuality and equality found between friends. We have only to recall the relationship between Teresa of Avila and John of the Cross, Peter Maurin and Dorothy Day, Dan Walsh and Thomas Merton, C. S. Lewis and Joy Davidman, the woman he first mentored and then married. Even the beautiful story of the Russian peasant and his *starets* in *The Way of a Pilgrim* reveals that death itself does not have to end the mentoring relationship, that one's mentor can continue to advise through significant dreams.

By now it should be clear that mentoring as a form of ministry is open to all, especially those who identify themselves as Christian. It is one of the most basic forms of love relationship, and we not only need mentors in our lives at various stages and life transitions, but we need to be mentors to others, particularly when we enter mid-life.

By briefly looking into the field of psychology, the world of myth and literature, and some of the vast history of Judeo-Christianity, we have gained a broader awareness of the many roles and dimensions of mentoring today. It is apparent, for example, that certain gifted people who acted as spiritual mentors profited from the influence of a mentor. Some of them also had a specific time of apprenticeship and special training with a mentor who taught them firsthand about the vocation itself. Today, training programs that include theological education, a history of spirituality, knowledge of psychology and supervised practicum can assist those who seek to enhance their gifts in mentoring and guidance. At the same time, whether or not we choose to act as a spiritual mentor in a more professional way, that ministry must not be seen as exclusive or elitist. It may, in fact, be done in the midst of other responsibilities and overlap other roles, as was the case with C. S. Lewis' various forms of mentoring. He can provide us with concrete examples of how "ordinary" mentoring in general and "spiritual" mentoring in particular can be a ministry that enhances the lives of others, as well as being an important resource for the development of our own spirituality. Let us turn to him for guidance.

TWO

C. S. Lewis as Spiritual Mentor

Friendship has been by far the chief source of my happiness.

C. S. Lewis, *Surprised by Joy*

More than 25 years after his death, C. S. Lewis has become one of the most popular Christian writers in the 20th century. His appeal transcends age, interests and theologies. Science fiction fans appreciate his novels; children's imaginations are touched by his *Narnia* tales; fundamentalists value his clear statements on Christianity; many find guidance from him regarding the meaning of suffering, the dimensions of grief and the ways of prayer. Lewis also speaks to those of us who study or teach theology, because he seems to consider theology itself not only as an intellectual journey (as important as that is) but also as a journey of the heart, a search for wisdom and the holy life. If we agree with Pascal's definition of a great person as someone who is not at one extremity or an-

37

other, but touches both at once, we can see in Lewis' broad appeal intimations of greatness.

I first came across the writings of C. S. Lewis in a bookstore in the mid-1970s. Somehow, up until then, I had not read anything by him. The first book I bought was *A Grief Observed*, and I took it back to my room and began to read it almost immediately. I was moved by the description of the loss of his wife, Joy Davidman, and recognized in his words dimensions of my own grief experiences over the years. He seemed to have the ability to name and clarify those experiences when he spoke of how our losses can have a powerful effect on our relationship with God; how they can often cause us, first, to wonder whether there is a God at all, or, if there is one, what sort of "cosmic sadist" he might be. More than any other book, Lewis' description of inner struggle and eventual surrender taught me how slow the process of grief can be, and how much care and respect we must give to it.

When I finished *A Grief Observed* I wanted to read more, and did. Again I found that Lewis was guiding me. At a time when I was struggling to comprehend why an older mentor seemed to be withdrawing from the important role he had taken on in my life, while a younger student whom I was mentoring began to seem so indifferent, I picked up Lewis' novel *Till We Have Faces*. While reading that re-telling of the ancient legend of Cupid and Psyche, I suddenly recognized that the dramatic story about Orual's possessiveness was mine as well. I came to realize that in the midst of anger, fear, self-doubt and guilt I had to let go of my expectations and the implicit demands I was making on those people whom I loved. Lewis helped me to see for the first time this dimension of my relationship with them, and of my need for loving them less selfishly. While that insight came as an act of grace, the process of letting go, of course, was much more painful and took a much longer time.

Lewis continued to guide me. In his autobiography, *Surprised by Joy*, I identified with his early love of books and literature, his passion for friendship as well as his wanting to be left alone, his resistance to allowing God to enter in. He introduced me to many English writers whose names I barely knew, as well as the writings of his own friends, the Inklings, whom I had not previously read.

Certainly one of his greatest contributions to me was introducing me to Oxford. Since first reading about Lewis' days there, and seeing pictures of Oxford in a book about his life, I wanted to visit that "sweet city," as he describes it in one of his early poems, "lulled by ancient streams."

I have now been to Oxford many times, including living there for a fall semester while doing research. On one of my visits, at the suggestion of Walter Hooper, Lewis' personal secretary, I took a bus to Headington, the suburb where Lewis and his wife, Joy, had once lived. After losing my way, I met a Mrs. Ellen Williams cutting grass out in front of one of the houses, only to discover that she had been a neighbor of theirs. Graciously inviting me, a total stranger, in for tea, she told me how unassuming Lewis had been and how surprised many of his neighbors were when the television show on his life, "Through the Shadowlands," revealed his many accomplishments and varied interests. "He never talked a lot about himself," she said. "We had no idea how important Lewis was, and how much influence he's had on so many people throughout the world." Then she led me up the road to his house, The Kilns, which at the time was unoccupied. In need of great repair, it seemed silent and abandoned. Yet as I attempted to imagine what it once had been like, and stared in through the living-room window at an empty room, I had the distinct impression of Lewis, once again sitting at his desk, looking back at me.

Obviously, I have been much impressed with his writings, but as I have gotten to know Lewis better through my research, I have discovered that there is more than just his appeal as a writer; there are also the very real accomplishments that can be found in his daily life and work. A professor of English literature at Oxford and Cambridge universities in England, he also acted as a lay theologian, preacher and spiritual guide. Believing that the church means the whole body of practicing Christians and that it is silly, even wrong to expect the clergy to do everything, Lewis demonstrated in many ways how mentoring, both "ordinary" and "spiritual," can be an important part of lay ministry.

This chapter explores three areas where he mentored others: through teaching, letter-writing and preaching. It attempts to discern what qualities and strengths he brought to these ministries and the implications of his mentoring for us who, whether professionally trained or not, see ourselves called to mentoring relationships, especially those associated with a specifically spiritual dimension.

C. S. Lewis as Tutor

The primary vocation out of which Lewis' extensive writings and all his ministries flowed was that of being a teacher. For over 30 years he taught students, most of that time at Magdalen College, Oxford. Lewis was part of the tutorial system found there, an approach to education in which, unlike American colleges where teaching primarily takes place in classrooms, a student is assigned a tutor with whom he or she meets each week in addition to attending lectures. During these tutorial sessions the student reads an essay composed the preceding week, and the professor offers comments and critique.

The published remarks of former students whom Lewis tutored provide insight into certain qualities that contributed to his effectiveness as a teacher, and witness to their own respect for and genuine love of the man. One of those students, H. M. Blamires, describes Lewis as someone who knew both how "to nourish a pupil with encouragement and how to press criticism when it was needed without causing resentment." Lewis did not think of himself "as taking pupils through a course; rather he saw his pupils as having two years or so under his guidance, during which they could start on a process which would occupy the responsive ones for the rest of their lives." Derek Brewer speaks of him as an ideal tutor—conscientious, efficient, intellectually brilliant, a man of wide culture. "One of his most notable characteristics," Brewer says, "was his magnanimity, his generous acceptance of variety and difference."

Luke Rigby, like Brewer, had Lewis as a tutor during World War II. He confirms Brewer's opinion, and then adds:

> What stands out in my memory is the warmth of the man.
> He was always welcoming and showed total interest and
> concern. The startling contrast between his achievement
> and my mediocre promise did not open a gulf; he was a true

master, the true teacher. He shared his appreciation and enthusiasm and thereby instilled confidence.

These brief comments are representative of many. When we study one of these tutoring relationships in more detail, we gain an even better understanding of Lewis as teacher and guide, and, as he himself moved toward conversion at the age of 31, of his ministry as a spiritual mentor.

One of the earliest students Lewis tutored at Oxford was Bede Griffiths, later to become a Benedictine monk and author of his own conversion story, *The Golden String*. Griffiths entered Magdalen College as an undergraduate in 1925, just after Lewis became a professor of English literature there. "Lewis was at this time," according to Griffiths, "no more Christian than I was." Though the younger man had no contact with Lewis his first two years, Lewis became his tutor during Griffiths' third year. Those weekly sessions in English literature revealed to the student some of his tutor's gifts:

> Lewis had the most exact and penetrating mind I had ever encountered, and his criticism of the essays which I had brought to him was the best education which I could have had. He had always a complete mastery of the subject, and never allowed any looseness of thought or expression. But these criticisms often led on to a general discussion, which was sometimes continued almost to midnight, and we began now to think along almost identical lines.

Lewis' mentoring gradually went beyond the subject of literature for, as Griffiths attests, while their relationship "ripened into friendship," it was through Lewis "that my mind was gradually brought back to Christianity." "Both he and I came to religion by way of literature," Griffiths acknowledges, and as they read together they "both began to discover more and more of the religious background of what we were reading."

Conversion did not happen suddenly for either of them, but involved a long process of shared questions and common readings in Chaucer, Spenser, Shakespeare, Milton, Wordsworth and Keats. While it was happening, Griffiths says, "I was probably nearer to Lewis than anyone else." When the younger man left Oxford still searching, the two continued to correspond by mail. Like the conversion stories of others before them, the turning point for both men came in solitude when they surrendered to a Higher Power, and knelt and prayed. Though Lewis was converted first, and though each man later came to identify his conversion with different ecclesial traditions, both describe their conversion in similar images and patterns.

In *Surprised by Joy*, the story of his conversion, Lewis speaks of his "mad wish" to call his soul his own. Finally, however, after years of searching, discussion and denial, he for the first time critically examines his life: "And there I found what appalled me; a zoo of lusts, a bedlam of ambitions, a nursery of fears, a harem of fondled hatreds. My name was legion." Later, alone in his room at Magdalen, he feels, night after night, "the steady, unrelenting approach of Him whom I so earnestly desired not to meet." What was demanded of him, he realized, was "total surrender, the absolute leap in the dark." And, in one of the most famous passages in the history of conversions, he tells us: "In the Trinity Term of 1929 I gave in, and admitted that God was God, and knelt and prayed: perhaps, that night, the most dejected and reluctant convert in all England." Whatever his initial feelings were, he was later able to acknowledge how "the hardness of God is kinder than the softness of men, and His compulsion is our liberation."

Within two years of Lewis' conversion Griffiths experienced his own form of liberation, what he identified as "the turning point of my life." It came in his London room when a great inner struggle began in which he was being called "to surrender the very citadel of myself." As the struggle continued for hours, Griffiths realized that "I had to surrender myself into the hands of power which was beyond my reason, which would not allow me to argue but commanded me to obey." In response to an inner voice demanding that he make a retreat (a term he wasn't acquainted with at the time), Griffiths found a place that offered one and then, for the first time, went to confession. He acknowledged to the priest how "I had turned my back on the truth," and then wept profusely: "Tears poured from my eyes, tears of the kind which I had never known before. My whole being seemed renewed.'' Returning to his room he opened the New Testament, read the words of St. John, and ''suddenly the meaning of what had happened dawned on my mind:''

> Through all these years I had thought that I had been seeking God. Now I suddenly saw that all the time it was not I who had been seeking God, but God who had been seeking me.

What is revealed in both men's stories is the similar steps or phases of conversion they followed: 1) years of searching, 2) a time of self-scrutiny or inventory, 3) the acknowledgment of sin, 4) surrender in solitude, and 5) an experience of God's overwhelming love for them despite their original reluctance, blindness or stubbornness. What is also striking is how each depended on the other for guidance and encouragement during those years of searching—even though Lewis had originally started as the older, more experienced, and more educated of the two. Lewis tells us in his autobiography that Griffiths was ''my chief companion on this stage of the road,'' and dedicates his book to his friend. Griffiths says that ''we were simply two friends finding our way to what was believed to be the truth.'' The younger man also points to some of the underlying dimensions of their relationship:

> He [Lewis] always treated me as an equal in every respect, as I believe that he treated all his other friends. In going through his correspondence with me, which covered more than thirty years, I have been touched to see how unvarying was his friendship, how totally he accepted me, appreciating what I said, disagreeing when necessary, but always with complete sincerity, giving his time and attention to answering my letters, as though he had nothing else to do. I think it was through him that I really discovered the meaning of friendship. There are not many things in my life more precious to me than that friendship.

C. S. Lewis as a Letter-Writer

That Lewis continued to correspond with Griffiths after the younger man had left Oxford was characteristic of him, for he consistently maintained relationships by mail when distance separated him from friends. As his fame grew through his books, however, the volume of mail from friends and strangers increased dramatically, and it became more difficult for him to keep up. Still, he answered the letters as soon as he could, sometimes with the help of his brother, Warren. Like John Henry Newman and Thomas Merton, Lewis' response to people in this way became another form of spiritual mentoring—encouraging and guiding others as they faced the questions of life and faith. Clyde Kilby, editor of some of those letters, tells us that the main reason Lewis answered them so conscientiously was that he believed "taking time out to advise or encourage another Christian was both a humbling of one's talents before the Lord and also as much the work of the Holy Spirit as producing a book." Another editor, James Como, describes Lewis as an "epistolist who steadily corresponded with literally thousands of strangers seeking advice and comfort," many of whom "attributed their religious conversions, reawakenings, and even vocations to Lewis' influence." One of these was Joy Davidman, the woman Lewis married late in life. Their relationship began as "pen-friends," after Lewis' writings had influenced Joy's own conversion.

Many of the thousands of letters Lewis wrote have been edited and published in separate volumes. All of them reveal a man of wide interests with a perceptive and sensitive nature, and the ability to laugh at himself. They also show a genuine concern for individual correspondents and a willingness to share the wisdom gained from personal experience and his own spiritual difficulties. In a letter to his godchild, Sarah, for example, he writes:

> Don't expect (I mean, don't count on and don't demand) that when you are confirmed, or when you make your first Communion, you will have all the feelings you would like to have. You may, of course: but also you may not. But don't worry if you don't get them. They aren't what matter. The things that are happening to you are quite real things whether you feel as you would wish or not.

Then he adds:

> This, by the way, is one of the very few subjects on which I
> feel I do know something. For years after I had become a
> regular communicant I can't tell you how dull my feelings
> were and how my attention wandered at the most important
> moments. It is only in the last year or two that things have
> begun to come right.

What is remarkable about his admission is that his letter to
Sarah was written some 20 years after his conversion—it was quite
some time before things began "to come right"!

Perhaps the most interesting correspondence in which Lewis
acted as spiritual mentor is found in *Letters to an American Lady*.
Here, unlike other books of his published letters, we can discern
the dynamics of an ongoing relationship with one person in particular and Lewis' response as guide. These letters were written to a
woman he had never met, a Roman Catholic widow, described by
those who knew her as a very charming and gracious Southern
aristocratic writer of articles, poems and stories. Because she
wished to remain anonymous when the letters were published, she
is referred to simply as "an American Lady." Lewis wrote to her
from 1950 to a few months before his death on November 22,
1963, and even though some of the letters are brief due to the pres-
sure of other responsibilities, Lewis' concern for the woman is evident. His letters reveal how spiritual mentoring, while it definitely includes discussion of the spiritual life, often goes beyond
so-called religious topics and God-talk. In them, Lewis discussed
everything with her from the price of books to his love for his
homeland, Ireland, and his numerous visits there: "All the mountains look like mountains in a story, and there are wooded valleys,
and golden sands, and the smell of peat from every cottage."

However, when she is faced with an unnamed "terrible afflic-
tion," Lewis is not afraid to offer serious advice: "The great
thing, as you have obviously seen (both as regards pain and finan-
cial worries), is to live from day to day and hour to hour not adding
the past or future to the present."

In another letter, he suggests that she avoid taking other people's inventories: "Try not to think—much less speak of their sins. One's own are a more profitable theme!" Concerning the paradox of ministry he tells her that "very often I expect, the service He really demands is that of *not* being (apparently) used, or not in the way we expected, or not in a way we can perceive." For the most part any advice he gives is presented in the context of his own life: "What most often interrupts my own prayers is not great distractions but tiny ones—things one will have to do or avoid in the course of the next hour."

This is perhaps the most common characteristic of Lewis' guidance: a willingness to share his sacred journey in all its joy and sorrow. Describing his life and others' as "a wandering to find home," he tells of his marriage in 1956 to Joy Davidman and how "no one can mark the exact moment at which friendship becomes love." He speaks of the adoption of Joy's two sons as his own and the adjustment that produced: "My brother and I have been coping with them for their Christmas holidays. Nice boys, but gruelling work for two old bachelors! I'm dead tired now." When his wife dies of cancer four years later, he acknowledges his sense of overwhelming loss and speaks of his own insights into the dimensions of grief: "It isn't a state, but a process. It keeps on changing—like a winding road with quite a new landscape at each bend." As his life draws to a close Lewis enunciates a principle underlying all mentoring: "We are members of one another whether we choose to recognize the fact or not." He also talks about an experience of personal conversion and reconciliation with a long-time (and long-dead) enemy:

> Do you know, only a few weeks ago I realized suddenly that I at last had forgiven the cruel schoolmaster who so darkened my childhood. I'd been trying to do it for years; and like you, each time I thought I'd done it, I found, after a week or so it all had to be attempted over again. But this time I feel sure it is the real thing. And (like learning to swim or to ride a bicycle) the moment it does happen it seems so easy and you wonder why on earth you didn't do it years ago.

His last letters to the American Lady allude to his own death and confirm his belief in resurrection. He tells her that "it will be fun when we at last meet," and, in farewell: "I am quite comfortable but easily tired. So you must expect my letters to be very few and very short. More a wave of the hand than a letter."

Sheldon Vanauken, author of *A Severe Mercy*, summarizes what many experienced through Lewis' letter-writing. For Vanauken Lewis was "a strong, genial, stimulating, loving presence in my life, above all, a friend." One other observation can be made. As much as Lewis' writing to people had a positive effect on their lives, he too learned, even to the point of incorporating that style of composition into two highly readable and successful books which took the form of letters. The first, *The Screwtape Letters*, ingeniously guides people on the dynamics of ongoing conversion; the second, *Letters to Malcolm: Chiefly on Prayer*, published posthumously, discusses, as he did with the American Lady, the dimensions of prayer, including its many distractions.

C. S. Lewis as Preacher

Not a great deal is written about Lewis as a lay preacher, especially when we consider the amount of space his biographers give to other aspects of his career. When we turn to some of Lewis' published remarks, as well as the recollections of friends, however, we discover how extensively he was involved in this form of spiritual mentoring. Not only did he preach at various Oxford and University of London chapels throughout his career, he also served during World War II on the staff of the Chaplains' Department of the Royal Air Force. This was at the time he was giving his ecumenical "Broadcast Talks" for the BBC explaining what he called "plain Christianity." Such involvement —in addition to his other professional responsibilities—might surprise us and even Lewis himself. As a friend of his recalled, "Lewis often said that if anyone had told him in his atheist days that he would someday step into a pulpit and preach he would have considered that man raving mad."

Those who heard Lewis preach relate how much they experienced his sermons as a form of personal guidance despite their being part of large, crowded congregations or a vast radio audience. A colleague of Lewis' at Oxford, Father Gervase Mathew, tells us that no matter what the occasion, Lewis always "forged a personal link with those who heard him." Erik Routley, a student at Oxford during the war years, suggests that so many people felt that linkage because of Lewis' personal attentiveness and serious concentration on his listeners when he spoke. According to Routley, this was Lewis' "great secret" and it explains why so many people had precious memories of him.

Stuart Babbage, a chaplain who arranged for Lewis to preach to servicemen, posits other reasons for Lewis' effectiveness as a preacher. In an excellent article, "To the Royal Air Force," Babbage says that it was due to Lewis' appreciation of imagery, metaphor and story; his speaking clearly and directly in "patterns of ordinary conversation"; and, his bringing into dialogue contemporary experience, literary sources, and Christian tradition in all its diversity. Most important, Babbage suggests, was Lewis' instinctive appreciation of empathy and self-identification. He knew how "to disarm his hearers by placing himself on the same level as those to whom he spoke." When preaching, for example, he preferred to wear an ordinary suit rather than some form of official garb. All this was not just a clever device or mere posturing: "Lewis was emphatic that he was neither a professional theologian nor a clergyman. He was, he insisted, a 'mere Christian,' " struggling like the rest of his listeners to understand and make sense of life and the Christian heritage.

These comments give us some insight into the dynamics behind the mentoring Lewis did through his preaching. We gain an even better understanding when we turn to the direct experience of two of those already quoted who heard him preach.

Routley, the student, was present on two occasions when Lewis preached in Oxford's Church of St. Mary the Virgin. Lewis' first sermon there, in the place where such notables as John Wesley and John Henry Newman also had preached, was delivered in the fall of 1939. That Lewis as a layman had been asked to preach at St. Mary's was evidently a public recognition of his varied talents in other areas, since Walter Hooper, his biographer, says that "perhaps the greatest accolade given Lewis" was this invitation. As Routley remembers the occasion:

> It was odd enough in those days to have a preacher there who wasn't a clergyman of the Church of England, and I thought I would go along. The service was held at 8:00 p.m. on Sunday, and I suppose I arrived about ten minutes before eight. There was hardly a seat to be had.

The young man's initial curiosity was rewarded, for he heard Lewis preach one of the great sermons of his career, "Learning in War-Time." "We are members of one body," Lewis told his congregation, "but differentiated members, each with his own vocation." Whatever our vocations might be, rooted as they are in our upbringing, talents, choices and circumstances beyond our control, all find their value in one principle: "The work of Beethoven, and the work of a charwoman, become spiritual on precisely the same condition, that of being offered to God, of being done humbly 'as to the Lord.' " Discerning our vocation also includes, Lewis said, leaving the future in God's hands:

> Never, in peace and war, commit your virtue or your happiness to the future. Happy work is best done by the man who takes his long-term plans somewhat lightly and works from moment to moment "as to the Lord." It is only our daily bread that we are encouraged to work for. The present is the only time in which any duty can be done or any grace received.

Routley returned to the university church in June 1941 to hear Lewis preach the sermon entitled "The Weight of Glory," described by two of Lewis' biographers as "perhaps the most sublime piece of prose" ever to come from his pen. Again, Routley tells us, "the place was packed solid before the service began," and yet, the manner in which Lewis "used words as precision tools, the effortless rhythm of sentences, the scholarship made friendly, the sternness made beautiful—these things all made it impossible for the listener to notice the passing of time." What especially touched his listeners was the power of Lewis' convictions, evident in the passage which is the origin of the sermon's title:

> It may be impossible for each to think too much of his own
> potential glory hereafter; it is hardly possible for him to
> think too often or too deeply about that of his neighbor. The
> load, or weight, or burden of my neighbor's glory should
> be laid daily on my back, a load so heavy that only humility
> can carry it. . . . There are no ordinary people. You have
> never talked to a mere mortal. . . . [I]t is immortals whom
> we joke with, work with, marry, snub, and exploit.

Then Lewis continues in a way highly characteristic of his personality and ministry:

> This does not mean that we are to be perpetually solemn.
> We must play. But our merriment must be of that kind (and
> it is, in fact, the merriest kind) which exists between people
> who have, from the outset, taken each other seriously—no
> flippancy, no superiority, no presumption. And our charity
> must be a real and costly love, with deep feeling for the sins
> in spite of which we love the sinner.

Routley left the church deeply moved by Lewis' poetry in the service of the gospel.

Stuart Babbage, the chaplain, gives us another account of Lewis' preaching, this time to a congregation not composed of young university students. In *C. S. Lewis: Speaker and Teacher*, he describes "one unforgettable night" when Lewis spoke to a select congregation of servicemen. As he tells the story, Lewis had been warned earlier that the officers and airmen to whom he would preach that evening would possibly face some form of ostracism from their more skeptical comrades for their participation in the religious service. Lewis had said then to Babbage that "it might be helpful it I told them something of what it costs me to be a Christian." That evening, with the Air Force chapel just as uncomfortably crowded as any Oxford church, Lewis evidently remembered his earlier conversation. As Babbage recalls the scene:

> Lewis stood in the aisle, a dishevelled and dumpy figure in
> a baggy suit. Having invoked the Name of the Father, the
> Son, and the Holy Spirit, he announced his text: "If any
> man will come after me, let him deny himself, and take up
> his cross, and follow me."

Lewis, so skillful in his use of metaphor and story, then went on to describe in vivid imagery the torture and brutal death of Jesus. He did not stop there, however, but brought the experience of Jesus into dialogue with his own:

> Lewis told us what it had cost him, as an Oxford don, to be a Christian. His liberal and rational friends, he explained, did not object to his intellectual interest in Christianity; but to insist on seriously practicing it—that was going too far. He did not mind being accused of religious mania, that familiar gibe of the natural man; what he was unprepared for was the intense hostility and animosity of his professional colleagues. Within the academic community, he unexpectedly found himself an object of ostracism and abuse.

Lewis related these hurtful memories, Babbage tells us, because of his concern for those who were listening to him, those who were also finding the Christian life difficult at times. Lewis also reminded them by way of concluding that all of this was not so unusual or unexpected if each of them recalled the original gospel story of a man who experienced new life in spite of suffering and even death.

The simplicity of Lewis' message and the personal witness he gave profoundly affected his listeners, according to Babbage, "for this was powerful preaching, born of intense and personally felt emotion." What contributed even more to the experience was Lewis' willingness to spend time, energy and himself visiting them "in the lonely wastes of the Norfolk fens" instead of staying safe within Oxford's hallowed halls. This itinerant ministry, travelling the length and breadth of England during wartime, revealed to Babbage Lewis' vast charity. He writes that Lewis, although a layman, had "a pastor's heart."

The Foundation of Lewis' Mentoring

Clearly Lewis was a very effective spiritual mentor, a layman of many gifts and qualities, all of which he brought to his ministry. Some of those qualities have already been named: his personal warmth and hospitality, his sense of humor and magnanimity, his willingness to share the wisdom gained from personal experience and reflection upon it. In retrospect perhaps Lewis' greatest quality, the one that connects all the others, was his care, a deep and abiding concern that Austin Farrer, a colleague and friend, described as Lewis' "taking of the world into his heart." This capacity for loving was manifest in his compassion and profound respect toward others. It was also evident in his genuine humility, that joyful acceptance of himself as a "mere Christian" who desired nothing more than to "compare notes" with others, as he says in *Reflection on the Psalms*, rather than "presuming to instruct." Most of all, when we consider all of Lewis' mentoring, this care was manifest in what his brother Warren called Lewis' remarkable talent for friendship. As our research shows, many people considered Lewis beyond his degrees and scholarly achievements (even in spite of them) as, quite simply, a friend. They saw him as someone who cared deeply about them, treated them as equals, and took them seriously—as he preached in his "Weight of Glory" sermon—without flippancy, superiority or judgment.

What was the origin of Lewis' care and his talent for friendship that many associated with his mentoring? Were the qualities he brought to his ministry given at birth or developed in time, the result of his environment or his own efforts? While we cannot answer those questions definitively, we can discern two distinct patterns in his life and ministry.

Without denying the charisms Lewis inherited at birth or developed in time, the first pattern we see is that his capacity for mentoring in many ways emerged because other people befriended and mentored him first. It is a pattern we discussed in Chapter 1, and one confirmed in the story of Lewis himself. Some of these mentors he met only through his love of books—people like George MacDonald, Spenser, Chesterton, Wordsworth, Blake. Other mentors were people with whom he lived and worked—people like Arthur Greeves, a life-long friend whom he called "my father confessor," who taught him the value of feelings; William Kirkpatrick, his private tutor during adolescence, who taught him to think critically; his wife, Joy, whom he called "my pupil and teacher," "my trusty comrade, friend," from whom he learned of the felicity that can come so unexpectedly when a friendship changes to passionate love; his group of friends, the Inklings, especially J.R.R. Tolkien and Charles Williams, who shared his love of writing and his need for male camaraderie. Even the violent teacher whom he calls Oldie in *Surprised by Joy*, the one he told the American Lady he had finally forgiven, taught him one of the most significant lessons of his life, that is, the kind of teacher and mentor he did *not* want to be, the kind of influence on others he did *not* want to have. Considering these diverse relationships we can agree with Lewis that "it takes all sorts to make a world, or a church," and, we might add, to shape a personality and form a friendly mentor.

Acknowledging the importance of these people, we can discern a second pattern in Lewis' life and ministry: Lewis' effectiveness as a spiritual mentor also came as a result of personal effort. "Nothing is any good until it has been down in the cellar for awhile," he once said, and it is evident in his writings that he took the time to reflect on his own experiences. Quite obviously he learned from that reflection about the value of care and friendship, and the need *for him* to mentor others. Such awareness and appreciation of friendship emerges as a major theme in his numerous works. His earliest poems, written after World War I and before his conversion to Christianity, speak of "our fellowship" being thinned "with many deaths," and of his hope for making new friends at his beloved Oxford:

> We are not wholly brutes. To us remains
> A clean, sweet city lulled by ancient streams,
> A place of vision and of loosening chains,
> A refuge of the elect, a tower of dreams.

In his first book after conversion, *Pilgrim's Regress*, Lewis writes of pilgrim John, his adventures with Mr. Vertue, Mother Kirk and the guide, like Lewis himself, whose "sight was so sharp that the sight of any others who travelled with him would be sharpened by his company." In *Four Loves*, containing his most complete theology of friendship, he says that friends are "travellers on the same quest," and, in agreement with the 12th-century monk

Aelred of Rievaulx, that true friendship is salvific, coming from
God as both a gift and a responsibility:

> Christ, who said to the disciples, "Ye have not chosen me,
> but I have chosen you," can truly say to every group of
> Christian friends, "You have not chosen one another, but I
> have chosen you for one another."

In his last book, *Letters to Malcolm: Chiefly on Prayer*, he
compares God to human friendship and speaks of the need for total
honesty when we pray:

> We must lay before God what is in us, not what ought to be
> in us. Even an intimate human friend is ill-used if we talk to
> him about one thing while our mind is really on another,
> and even a human friend will soon become aware when we
> are doing so.

Judging from Lewis' numerous writings on that theme, as well as
his many friendships, it is no wonder that he tells us in *Surprised
by Joy* that "friendship has been by far the chief source of my happiness." It was also the foundation of his mentoring.

A story told by Clifford Morris expresses not only how Lewis'
friendship and care were often linked in people's minds, but also
how Lewis believed friendship itself, like prayer, is based upon
trust and speaking the truth to one another:

> I remember that I once wanted to speak to him (Lewis)
> about something that was in the nature of a very personal
> and delicate matter, and he must have sensed my diffi-
> dence. I shall never forget how he turned to me, how he
> smiled at me, and how he then said with tremendous affec-
> tion, "My dear Morris, friends can say anything to one an-
> other, and be quite sure that no confidence will be broken."
> His written words—so deservedly popular—and his spoken
> words to private individuals—so remembered and
> cherished—were freely given, but not without care.

As Morris' story reveals, and Lewis' other relationships confirm, Lewis as spiritual mentor encouraged and invited people to
speak from the heart, to speak openly and honestly about them-

selves in ways that often led to greater depth in the relationship as well as in many cases to conversion, a change of heart. John Henry Newman equated friendship with "heart speaking to heart," and in the history of Christian spirituality it is one of the most ancient and valued practices. The desert fathers and mothers believed that this *exagoreusis*, opening one's heart, leads to *hesychia*, inner peace of heart. John Cassian, writing in the fifth century, speaks of its healing power: "The foul serpent from the dark underground cavern must be released; otherwise it will rot." Carl Jung, writing in the twentieth century, would agree with Cassian on the need for self-revelation, but he also was convinced that any guidance that leads to healing or transformation depends not only on the honest communication between people but on the wisdom and care of the guide: "The practice of this art lies in the heart; if your heart is false, the physician within you will be false."

Now we begin to see why Farrer referred to Lewis' friendship and care in terms of the heart. The qualities Lewis brought to his ministry, especially his care, had a transforming effect on people, helping many to discern a direction in their lives as well as the presence of a caring God who is with us as friend and companion on our journeys. Such charisms used for community service have often been associated in the past with the power of ordination. The chaplain Babbage, for example, quoted earlier, compared Lewis' care to his having a pastor's heart. What Lewis' ministry teaches us, however, is that one does not have to be ordained to manifest a care called pastoral. It is not only the ordained who have the power to effect dramatic change. As Chad Walsh writes in *Light on C. S. Lewis* when discussing one form of Lewis' mentoring: "Though no bishop ever laid hands upon his head, he was a genuine pastoral counselor via the postal system to many fellow pilgrims who perhaps never sat in the study of an ordained minister." In some mysterious way, all Lewis' forms of spiritual mentoring transcended the distinctions between those who are or are not ordained, revealing that there is no greater ministry than that advocated by Christ: "I call you friends; love one another as I have loved you" (cf. Jn 15:12-17).

Implications for Mentoring

What are the implications of Lewis' mentoring for our own ministries? What are some lessons he as spiritual mentor can teach us, a people of a different age and members of a seemingly more complex society and church?

First, Lewis can help us recognize the importance of friendship as the foundation of any mentoring we do. We may not have Lewis' talents and qualities, but all of us, made in God's image, have the capacity to reach out with care, to offer others our friendship when it is appropriate to do so. The interrelationship between friendship and mentoring is affirmed not only by Lewis' ministry, but as we have already seen, by such people as Yale psychologist Daniel Levinson and by such groups as Alcoholics Anonymous. Thomas Merton, echoing the words of Lewis to Morris, describes the spiritual director as primarily a friend with whom we can say "what we really mean in the depths of our souls, not what we think we are expected to say."

Second, as Lewis' mentoring reveals, it is often difficult to distinguish spiritual mentoring from other forms. While the spiritual mentor's relationship may be characterized by more depth and may be focused more on the spiritual dimensions of life, such as conversion, vocation and the quality of our relationships with neighbor and God, it is often closely intertwined with other forms of mentoring like teaching, sponsoring or counselling. As Lewis' relationship with Bede Griffiths shows, spiritual mentoring may occur only because other forms of mentoring have preceded it. Perhaps the real difference between spiritual mentoring and other forms is related more to the Christian beliefs and vision the spiritual mentor brings to the relationship than to any difference in specific functions. If we agree with Lewis that "there is no essential quarrel between the spiritual life and the human activities as such," we can see that to exclude any of the ordinary activities of "mere Christianity" is to deny the fundamental goodness of creation, the unity of our humanity-divinity and the sacredness of our journeys through time.

Third, Lewis' ministry teaches us that our spiritual mentoring can take many forms. It need not be limited to one-on-one relationships, but can also include large groups inside or outside liturgical settings. What is important in spiritual mentoring is our conviction that mentoring is valuable and that through our pastoral care we are able to forge a link with others and speak a language of the heart.

Fourth, Lewis' mentoring reminds us that any link between ourselves and others depends on our willingness and courage to share our lives and stories—not as people with all the answers, but as those who are searching also for wisdom in the midst of multiple responsibilities and uncertainties. Lewis' sermon to the Norfolk airmen bears this out: honestly sharing our struggles and dreams brings us closer to one another. As Lewis said so often, "We are members of one another"; the sharing of our stories consistently confirms that fact.

Fifth, although we are not necessarily as talented as Lewis, we all have the ability and responsibility to identify and develop the qualities we do have. We can do this in the same way Lewis did: by taking the time to reflect on our experiences and the questions that they raise. This reflection is not only theology in its most basic sense as "faith seeking understanding," but also a form of prayer, which can become a daily practice and discipline. Through our contemplation we might develop an ever-deepening gratitude and wonder for all those who have loved us first—long before we had awakened to a Higher Power of Love. We might begin to see what they have contributed, and what we, in turn, can contribute to other lives. Such "going down into the cellar" might even help us begin to accept and celebrate *both* our strengths and limitations, in their totality, as resources for our ministry.

Sixth, Lewis' many significant relationships demonstrate how all mentoring, especially spiritual mentoring, is a form of empowerment that helps others discern their vocations, acknowledge their gifts and begin to give shape to their dreams. As Lewis' and Griffiths' relationship also reveals, there is a paradox present in such empowering. Helping others discern their call and encouraging them to risk changes can affect the mentor as much as the person being mentored. In a very real way mentoring contributes to each person's ongoing conversion and discernment of vocational response. This mutuality in mentoring, so often experienced by those who call themselves friends, affirms the most fundamental belief of all Christians: it is not Christianity in the abstract that saves, but Christianity in the flesh.

Finally, Lewis teaches us that genuine mentoring transcends space and time. An encounter with a mentor is not dependent on physical meetings, but rather on the deepest level of communication: the communion of souls. This communion of souls is clearly demonstrated in all Lewis' mentoring relationships, most especially with the American Lady. In retrospect, we can see that though they never met—in a very real sense they did.

Lewis as Soul Friend

Besides what we can learn from Lewis' life and writings about mentoring, there is a Celtic spiritual tradition that can give us more insight. Celtic people, the Irish in particular, have always valued friendship as an important and lasting relationship. The ancient Irish, in fact, had a word for someone who acts as a spiritual mentor in a relationship of great depth. The word is *anamchara*, "soul friend," someone who joyfully embraces our life, questions and suffering as an extension of his or her own; someone with whom we can speak the language of the heart; someone, as Augustine defines true friendship, one's soul cannot be without. In the next chapter we will examine some of the history of this tradition and some of its implications for ourselves.

C. S. Lewis stands in this Celtic spiritual tradition of mentoring. Many of us who read his books or the stories about him encounter a close friend who opens windows on our souls revealing *our* belief in the ministry of all the baptized, *our* search for a united Church that values the gifts of everyone, *our* need for friendships and genuine community.

To propose Lewis as a model of spiritual mentoring is in no way to deny his human limitations. As various of his friends admit, Lewis could be stubborn when he thought he was right and intolerant of certain aspects of modern life that we might consider essential to an informed citizenry. He refused, for example, to listen to a radio or read a daily newspaper, stating that if anything were important enough someone would tell him. His views on women and the headship of families—at least until he met and married Joy Davidman—would be considered by many today as archaic, if not outright sexist. Still his gifts far surpassed his limitations, and even some of those limitations can be seen, like our own, as the reverse side of certain strengths. Whether or not we agree with all of Lewis' opinions, many of us perceive him as did a Cambridge scientist who met him for the first time, as "a very good man, to whom goodness did not come easily." In that recognition we are given hope in our own struggle to live holy lives.

Anyone who considers Lewis a soul friend and visits his beloved Oxford experiences his presence in certain places: Magdalen College where he tutored and wrote so many letters, the Church of St. Mary the Virgin where he preached, the Eastgate Hotel where he first met Joy Davidman, the Eagle and Child Pub where he and the Inklings met each week. While the words of Shakespeare, "Men must endure their going hence," imprinted so starkly on Lewis' tomb in the country churchyard, remind us of the reality of death and of our mortality, those other places and Lewis' own words remind us of a greater reality: Friendships survive death itself. As he wrote in his last book:

> Then the new earth and sky, the same yet not the same as these, will live in us as we have risen in Christ. And once again, after who knows what aeons of the silence and the dark, the birds will sing and the waters flow, and the lights and shadows move across the hills, and the faces of our friends laugh upon us with amazed recognition.

THREE

The Irish Soul Friend

> Go off and don't eat until you get a soul friend, because
> anyone without a soul friend is like a body without a head.
> The water of a limey well is not good to drink nor good for
> wishing. It is like a person without a soul friend.
>
> St. Brigid to a cleric, *Book of Leinster*

Robert Bellah's *Habits of the Heart* contends that contemporary Americans are suffering from an overemphasis on individualism and need to recover not only a language of community and commitment but also knowledge of their traditions. "Our lives make sense," Bellah states, "in a thousand ways, most of which we are unaware of, because of traditions that are centuries, if not millennia, old. It is these traditions that help us to know that it does make a difference who we are and how we treat one another." The discovery of some of our mentoring traditions may enrich both our spirituality as Americans and our ministry as spiritual friends. One of the traditions intimately connected with the ministry of spiritual mentoring is that of the Irish *anamchara* or soul friend.

I first heard the word *anamchara* at the University of Notre

Dame during a course on the sacrament of penance. The word
caught my attention and continued to intrigue me, would not let me
be. As Lewis' books had first named my experiences associated
with grief, this word and the spiritual tradition associated with it
named certain experiences of reconciliation and relationships of
spiritual mentoring in my life. I recalled my adult conversion experience with Joe, the relationships I had with my supervisors
Gordie and Frank during my clinical training year, the spiritual
mentoring I was then receiving from Fritz, especially regarding
my dreams. The more I studied the tradition of the *anamchara* the
more I came to realize how much it might help others name their
experiences of healing and forgiveness, and the ministry in which
so many are already participating.

The spiritual tradition of the *anamchara* is one part of a larger
history of spiritual mentoring, a history of great wealth and great
diversity. This history includes all those wisdom figures mentioned earlier, people like Jerome, who advises a friend not to set
out into the unknown without a guide; Teresa of Avila, who
stresses the need for a director who is experienced in the spiritual
life; Aelred of Rievaulx, who equates our spiritual friendships
with our search for wisdom and ultimately our relationship with
God. "Friendship is nothing else but wisdom," Aelred writes in
Spiritual Friendship, and "he that abides in friendship, abides in
God, and God in him."

While many specific examples are found in history and in the
classical works of wisdom figures within our spiritual heritage,
the tradition of the Irish *anamchara* has been largely ignored by
church historians, theologians and spiritual writers. Two noted
scholars of Irish history, John T. McNeill and Kathleen Hughes,
refer to the *anamchara* only in passing. The English spiritual
writer Kenneth Leech entitles his popular book on spiritual direction *Soul Friend*, but devotes only a few pages to that Irish tradition from which his book takes its name. Brian Patrick McGuire's
monumental book *Friendship and Community: The Monastic Experience, 350-1250* has even less material on that specific tradition
of friendship.

As a form of spiritual mentoring, however, the ministry of the

Irish *anamchara* significantly affected not only the evolution of the sacrament of reconciliation in the Western church, but also, as noted spiritual theologians Jean Leclercq and Louis Bouyer acknowledge, the whole growth of Christian spirituality. According to Leclercq and Bouyer, this ministry affirmed "a feeling in man that his relations with God can take the form of effective dialogue," and because of that conviction all of Christian spirituality has been transformed. Christians began to realize much more explicitly as a result of their relationships with soul friends that words shared in honesty and openness transform those involved in the encounter—and make it possible for them to encounter God.

Before discussing some of the rich spiritual heritage associated with the *anamchara* and what certain Irish saints can teach us about this important form of spiritual mentoring, let us first put it in the context out of which it emerged: a spirituality rooted in the soil and history of Ireland itself.

Ireland's Spirituality: Experiences That Shape

Every people has a history, a culture, a spirituality manifest in daily, often unperceived routines, special events celebrated communally, a particular way of acknowledging the sacred and a relationship with the Holy One. This way of life, this spirituality, is passed on from generation to generation as the young hear stories from their parents of the griefs and triumphs of their ancestors, of the traditions that are theirs, and how those familial traditions affect their own identities. In many ways all people are alike: They laugh at the humorous and ridiculous, they cry out at the tragic and absurd, they share a common story of births and deaths, conflicts and maturations. Their lives are filled with sacred and awesome memories, sometimes unrealistic and yet often fulfilled dreams. They are cared for when they are young, and they learn, if they are blessed, of the importance of caring for others in return. These are some similarities humanity shares.

There are differences too: a diversity of personalities, nations and cultures that contribute to the rich colors and textures of humankind's unfolding tapestry. Two important factors that add to the differences of a people's spiritual heritage are its geography and the specific events of its history. Anyone who has visited Ireland or become acquainted with its history knows how those factors have directly affected the people of Ireland, now numbering almost five million, and perhaps also those whose heritage is there.

Geographically Ireland is located to the west of Britain, a land to which it was attached before the Ice Age. Four times larger than Sicily and Sardinia, yet somewhat smaller than Iceland or Cuba, it is an island surrounded by the Irish Sea and the Atlantic Ocean. Its location has contributed to its moderate climate, which has affected the spectacular beauty of the land. The Irish are known for their love of nature and their appreciation of creation. It is a characteristic of their spirituality that goes back into the mists of time, an appreciation certainly acknowledged by the early Celts and their religious leaders, the druids, when they chose to build their high altars in the midst of sacred groves of ivy and oak. This same appreciation was passed on to the early Irish church as an evolution of spirituality arising out of its own history and culture rather than one transplanted from somewhere else.

Ireland has been given the name the Emerald Isle. Its green fields are often interrupted only by the horizons of a blue sky or sudden showers of rain upon an open field; its green foliage by multicolored fuchsias and purple rhododendron; its green meadows by bright yellow gorse and stone walls with many shades of gray. In the summertime purple and pink heather can be seen on the mountaintops near the lakes of Killarney and the Ring of Kerry bordering the sea. Being so close to that broad expanse of water, its depths, its tides, the pounding of white-crested surf can elicit in a person the sense of creation's overwhelming power. Its brooding, lonely emptiness makes a people receptive to mysticism, romantic excess and dreams. Where the land ends and horizons fade away, people experience transcendence too. Creation itself opens one's eyes to the Creator, leads one to an experience of awe and gratitude, invites a person to begin to search for a loving, creative power whose presence is felt in one's very fiber, whose power is physically visible to the naked eye. Such geographical beauty with its accompanying sense of awe has contributed to the Irish people's appreciation of poetry, music and dance. One can see why the writer, Sean O'Faolain, writes that the Irish person's idea of heaven "is free of time but it is rooted in Place," and describes Ireland itself as "this island of dark green brooding under a sky that is one vast pearl." And why James Joyce could speak of his heart dancing like "a cork upon a tide."

A second major factor which has influenced and continues to affect the spirituality of Ireland is its long and tragic history. As Stephen Dedalus in *Ulysses* says, "History is a nightmare from which I am trying to awake." Ireland is a story, many stories, of encounters with powerlessness, poverty and persecution. Some of these encounters have been brought on by the Irish people's own creative, romantic, highly individualistic natures, which found it difficult in the ancient past to unite as tribes against a common foe and in the present to cooperate as one people building one nation. Unfortunately there is some truth to Samuel Johnson's remark to Boswell that "the Irish are a fair people; they never speak well of one another." That saying finds balance in the old Irish proverb, "Contention is better than loneliness." Beyond these characteristics is the presence in Ireland's history of those euphemistically referred to as strangers. These were the people who literally would not leave the island alone, and while they contributed gifts of cities and language, they also intensified the feelings of powerlessness, the experiences of poverty and the persecutions that continue to divide and alienate, fostering ongoing hatred and despair. The autobiography of Bobby Sands, who died while on a hunger strike in 1981, vividly portrays not only the violence perpetrated against him and other prisoners seeking a united Ireland, but also the vicious cycle in which the perpetrators, the pro-British guards, are themselves trapped. Out of these generation-to-generation, day-to-day relationships of injustice and inequality, two Irelands emerged and presently exist: the Republic of Eire in the south and Northern Ireland. All of these experiences, modern and ancient, find expression today in the haunting lyrics of such songs as "Four Green Fields" and "A Nation Once Again."

Ironically, it is this history of tragedy and survival that gives the Irish an appreciation for family ties and family stories, and for the virtues of humor and hospitality. When we endure poverty, hunger and suffering, we naturally turn to our families for comfort and support; when we stand against injustice, all those who share our vision of righting wrongs become our allies; when we consistently face frustrations and disappointments, we learn to either laugh or cry. The Irish know how to celebrate the good times as well as the bad. They come together as family to celebrate baptisms, marriages, wakes. Their stories, music, dancing and poetry express the gratitude for what has been given and their attempt to accept loss and the tragic dimension of all human life. That is the positive side of what powerlessness, poverty and persecution have wrought. However, the same overwhelming oppression that can lead to compassion, sensitivity and the celebration of life's richness has also led at times to the dark side of the Irish experience: the escape into alcoholism, superstition, blind dependency on the church, or a despair that recognizes no loving God. Like F. Scott Fitzgerald's book, the Irish story consists of both the beautiful and the damned. An important part of that story, however, which speaks of the creative and compassionate side of Irish history and spirituality, is that associated with the *anamchara* or soul friend.

Christian Origins of the Irish Soul Friend

The ministry of the *anamchara* originated in one of the oldest churches of Christianity. Long before ecclesial divisions pulled that sacred reality apart, a different kind of Christian faith arose in Ireland, Scotland, Wales, northern England, Cornwall and Brittany, those countries influenced by a pagan Celtic culture that preceded Christianity. This particular form of distinctly Celtic Christian faith resulted in a rare flowering of creativity at a time when the rest of Europe was experiencing what historians have named the Dark Ages. Celtic Christianity, finding expression especially in Ireland, became identified with poetic imagination, self-determination, local ecclesial autonomy and an appreciation of women's gifts. It developed for centuries largely outside of the influence and structures of the church in Rome, taking shape in monasteries populated not only by ascetic idealists, but by entire families. These monastic communities became centers of learning, storytelling and art, as well as pastoral centers where healing, hospitality and soul friendship were available to pilgrims, students, scholars and penitents alike. Celtic Christianity also found expression in high crosses, round towers, illuminated gospels and the love of stories shared.

This early Irish church had a significant effect on the other churches, notably in its *anamchara* relationships, which affected the evolution of the sacrament of reconciliation in the Western church, eventually supplanting the earlier communal reconciliation rites. To understand the various dimensions of the ministry of the soul friend in the early Irish church, we need to take a brief look at the *anamchara's* Christian origins.

What we find in the earliest years of the Christian story after Christ are communities of primarily adult converts, highly conscious as mature people of the possibility of human failures and recurring sin. Seeking to support their new way of life, they came to value certain communal customs that reinforced their ongoing conversion process, especially those related to ministry and prayer: performing works of mercy and charity and breaking bread together in Jesus' name (Acts 2:42). Part of that early communal life was also the practice of gentle confrontation (Gal 6:1-2), as well as confessing their problems and sins to one another (Jas 5:16-20). This form of lay confession and guidance surely included helping one another discern the loving presence and healing power of God in their midst. As friends in Christ they also must have assured each other that their God, despite sins and failures, was always ready to forgive. More serious sins like adultery, murder and apostasy had to be dealt with more drastically since they threatened the life of the community itself, but even for those expelled due to such serious sins a rehabilitation process offered hope of being welcomed back. This latter pastoral practice eventually evolved into a three-part process consisting of the confession of sin to a bishop or presbyter, doing acts of penance with a group of peers for an extended period of time, and finally being reconciled with the community in a public celebration of thanksgiving.

The emergence of soul friendship in Ireland—a more specialized form than that of the common early Christian practice of

confrontation, confession and guidance—has historical links
with certain gifted individuals found in fourth and fifth century
Egypt, Syria and Palestine. These desert fathers (*abbas*) and
mothers (*ammas*) sought a special relationship of intimacy with
God by going into the desert wilderness, away from the decay
and overcrowding of city life and the disintegration of the civili-
zation to which they belonged. These spiritual guides became
known for their holiness and spiritual wisdom, their knowledge
of the heart. Since good news travelled as quickly then as it does
now, many others disillusioned with their age and also seeking
wisdom sought them out for guidance and spiritual mentoring.
This spiritual mentoring included both the acknowledgement of
sin and the discernment of God's spirit in the heart, a form of lay
confession, since those consulted were most often not ordained.
They believed, as was mentioned earlier, that the opening of
one's heart to another, what they called *exagoreusis*, leads to *hesychia* or peace of heart. Knowledge of this practice of spiritual
counseling and healing was eventually brought to Ireland by literary sources and quite possibly by those who had visited the desert and consulted with spiritual guides or their proteges. As a
ministry combined with that of the early pagan Celtic druids—the
teachers, counselors and reconcilers of their tribes—Christian
anamcharas began to flourish on the Emerald Isle when the great
missionary-bishop Patrick brought Christianity to Ireland in
A.D. 432.

  When considering Patrick we need to see him not only as a
genuine historical figure, but also as one whose life is wrapped in
legends and the larger truths of myth. He is a representative person
whose story represents the numerous unknown monks and missionaries who travelled throughout the Western world and who
had been at work and at prayer in Ireland even before Patrick arrived. Nevertheless, Patrick's story is inspiring, especially when
the British-born saint describes his call to return to the land where
he had been held captive as a youth. Like many, his vocation was
evidently discerned in the language and mystery of dreams, for we
find in the autobiographical writings that he left us the following
account:

I saw, in the bosom of the night, a man coming as it were, from Ireland . . . with letters . . . and he gave one of them to me. And I read the beginning of the letter containing "the voice of the Irish" . . . and they cried out then as if with one voice "We entreat thee, holy youth, that thou come, and henceafter walk among us."

Because of Patrick's response to his dreams and the labors of so many before and after him, Ireland was converted to Christianity, and an Irish church came into being. This church was primarily made up of monastic communities, by size sometimes monastic cities, such as Glendalough in the Wicklow Mountains or Clonmacnoise on the banks of the Shannon River. These early monasteries were presumably of the Egyptian type, which had first appeared in western Britain in the fifth century. However, according to historians Maire and Liam de Paor:

The tendency towards monasticism already existed in Ireland. . . . The Irish social system with its emphasis on kinship and personal rule readily received the concept of the monastic family with its abbot. . . . The old sea route to western France and the Mediterranean—the route of the wine trade—almost certainly remained open in spite of the barbarians and it seems likely that there were some direct contacts between Ireland and Egypt.

In whatever way monasticism reached Ireland and whoever brought it there, with it came the practice and relationship of spiritual mentoring, which had flourished in the desert.

There in the land of Clonfert, Cashel, Kells, Kildare and Dysert O'Dea this form of confession-discernment-guidance developed and spread. Evidently not limited in its creative origins only to the ordained or only to men, this form of spiritual mentoring can be seen as a significant part of what historians have come to call the flowering of Ireland. For nearly six centuries, from the late 500s to the 1100s, and especially in the Golden Age of the seventh and eighth centuries, Ireland became a beacon of light in the midst of a darkening Western world. It was during the Dark Ages that Ireland experienced a time of great creativity in education, the arts of

metal and illuminated gospels, and spirituality. There in the forests of Monasterboice, by the lakes of Glendalough, on the steep
and jagged slopes of Skellig Michael, near the windswept isles of
the Killarney lakes, this rare flowering took shape, and relationships of soul friends developed. Because the pagan Celts respected
women as equals before Christianity came to Ireland, it seems that
the ministry of the *anamchara* included Christian women. St.
Brendan, for example, had St. Ita of Cluain Credill, a virgin and
teacher, as a spiritual mentor and confessor. According to two
writers on the practice of Celtic penance, Thomas Murphy and
Michael Rankin, "As in the East, the lines separating confessors
who are priests and those who are not ordained are by no means
clearly perceived."

Many women in the early Irish church, in fact, followed a monastic life. There were major monasteries of women at Killeedy,
Killevy, Clonbroney and Kildare. The earliest abbess of Kildare,
Brigid, is considered—along with Patrick and Columcille—one of
Ireland's greatest saints; she ruled her double-monastery, consisting of both women and men, with an authority, some said, equal to
a bishop's. Even when the members of the communities were exclusively male, women in the early Irish church were not afraid to
speak their minds. In *The Life of Senan*, one of the Irish saints, we
find the story of a woman who wanted to take up the religious life
with Senan on his island near the entrance to the Shannon harbor.
The saint, we are told, was reluctant to admit her, but she was not
put off. She tells him directly in words that continue to challenge
us today: "Christ is no worse than you. Christ came to save
women no less than men. He suffered for the sake of women no
less than for men. Women have given service and ministry to
Christ and his apostles. Women enter the heavenly kingdom no
less than men." Senan heard and, moved by her honesty and conviction, welcomed her to his retreat.

With both women and men participating in the ancient practice found in the desert, soul friendships became refined in the
Emerald Isle. For years the people of Ireland participated in
those relationships of self-disclosure and guidance. The practice
was carried to Britain and the rest of the European continent

when Irish missionaries travelled abroad. It was also encountered by many other Christians who came to study in Ireland, as the Venerable Bede attests in his *History of the English Speaking People*:

> At this time there were many in England, both nobles and commons, who, in the days of Bishops Finan and Colman, had left their own country and retired to Ireland either for the sake of religious studies or to live a more ascetic life. In course of time some of these devoted themselves faithfully to the monastic life, while others preferred to travel round to the cells of various teachers and apply themselves to study. The Irish welcomed them all gladly, gave them their daily food, and also provided them with books to read and with instruction, without asking for any payment.

This form of spiritual mentoring gained in popularity as more people found it helpful for their ongoing conversion and spiritual growth. Although initially opposed by Roman church authorities, spiritual mentoring eventually came to be recognized as a necessary part of Christian spirituality. In 1215 participation in these encounters *with a priest* was made obligatory at the Fourth Lateran Council. Later, at the Council of Trent in the 1500s, these holy encounters were institutionalized, legally defined as one of the seven great sacraments of the Roman church—the sacrament of reconciliation, popularly referred to as confession before Vatican II.

To gain more insight into the *anamchara* relationship and spiritual mentoring, let us turn to some ancient stories of the Irish saints. Like the legends associated with St. Patrick, these stories contain many mythological elements that in no way can be interpreted as historically accurate. They do, however, reveal a great deal of psychological and spiritual wisdom about human nature and our relationship with God.

Lives of Irish Soul Friends

In addition to monastic rules, penitentials, devotional and liturgical compositions, letters and chronicles, one of the main classes of texts that shed more light on the soul friend heritage is the *acta sanctorum*, or lives of the saints. These hagiographies were influenced a great deal by the scriptures, the writings of Jerome, John Cassian, Gregory the Great, and other lives, such as Athanasius' *Life of Antony*, a desert father, and Sulpicius Severus' *Life of St. Martin*, a popular bishop of Tours in Gaul. One of the major sources of Irish hagiography, *Lives of Irish Saints*, was compiled and translated by Oxford scholar Charles Plummer and first published in 1922. These lives are based on legends that go back as far as the sixth century, although they often seem to portray an ecclesial system more Roman and a culture more medieval than the earliest days in the Irish church after Patrick. However, they are firsthand sources for the history of the legends and cults of the saints, those friends of God who became for many others soul friends.

The ten Irish saints whose lives are found in Plummer's book are referred to as "the Great Monastic Founders." Historically they are members of "the Second Order of Irish saints," those who were not contemporaries of St. Patrick, but of the generation that followed. A number of them are included among "the twelve apostles of Ireland," proteges of the great teacher Finnian of Clonard, whose soul friend and mentor was St. David of Wales. To enter the world of Plummer's saints is to encounter kings of tribes, bishops of dioceses, "abbots" of Rome, witches and druids, sea monsters and red dragons, hosts of angels and even (perhaps not surprisingly) demons "in the shapes of dwarfs and leprechauns whose faces were black as coal." Unlike the *abbas* and *ammas*, these Irish saints did not go into the barren wilderness of the deserts; they are found near blue-green lakes or within dark forests or in the shadows of heather and gorse-covered mountaintops. Unlike the desert spiritual guides who, following the example of St. Antony, at first sought solitude as hermits, these Irish saints seem for the most part determined to found monastic communities for the glory of God. Unlike the desert guides, who tended to settle in one place for the rest of their lives, these Irish pioneers were true missionaries and pilgrims, imitators of Patrick and Brendan. They did, however, often reside in hermitages or cells, at least for a while and, as one of the lives of Ciaran of

Saighir reveals, practiced an asceticism similar to the desert fathers and mothers:

> And these were the virtuous customs of Ciaran all his life;
> he never wore woollen clothing, but skins of wolves and
> other brute beasts; and he avoided all dainty meats, all in-
> toxicating drinks; and he took but little sleep.

These Irish saints, recognized for their wisdom, also had a miraculous ability to heal and even raise people from the dead. They had a special affinity with animals such as deer, fox, otters, salmon and even wolves. The heroic dimensions of some of these saints were also, shall we say, somewhat exceptional. We are told, for example, that Ruadan was 12 feet tall, and that Mochuda was unusually handsome. "Thirty maidens loved him so passionately that they could not conceal it." Mochuda handled this dilemma in his own way! As the story goes:

> This was grievous to Mochuda, and he prayed to God to
> turn this love into a spiritual love, and He did so. And
> Mochuda made nuns of these maidens, and they were serv-
> ing God till they died.

These saints were known for being holy men and women of God— even good cooks—and in their compassion, patience and love we can discern great generativity. Perhaps the most interesting symbolic portrayal of such generativity is found in the *Life of Colman Ela*, who had "two paps such as no saint ever had before, a pap with milk, and a pap with honey," which nourished two fosterlings under his care. Still, the reader sometimes senses that it is not so much moral goodness, but the possession of some magical power to work miracles that seems so important in the saints' ministries. It is as if the pre-Christian "magic potency of the druid" is reflected in their stories—as it surely is, especially when these saints are portrayed as pronouncing numerous psalms of cursing and vengeance upon their enemies, an ancient Celtic druid practice. When it came to writing their obituaries, however, their admirers called upon their own Judeo-Christian heritage of stories and images, as well as a bit, perhaps, of Irish blarney. As the *Life of Bairre of Cork* effuses:

> He was a true pilgrim like Abraham; he was compassion-
> ate, simple, and forgiving of heart like Moses; he was a
> treasury of wisdom and knowledge like Solomon; he was a
> man full of grace and favour of the Holy Spirit, like the
> youth John.

For a full page the attributes go on: He was a serpent for cunning, a dove in gentleness, a crystal fountain, a heavenly cloud, a golden lamp, a shining fire, a precious stone and, most interesting if one considers the desert tradition of equating spiritual guidance with healing, "the true leech who healed sicknesses and disease of the body and soul of every believer in the Church."

But what do the Irish saints specifically teach us about the *anamchara* relationship?

While there are numerous stories in Plummer's book related to that form of spiritual guidance and confession, let us refer to just a few and note some of the patterns they reveal.

In the *Life of Brendan of Clonfert* we discover that every soul friend needs another with whom to pray, to seek advice and to help discern the sometimes imperceptible movements of the heart. Brendan, we are told, has a great love for the Lord "in his heart" and decides to "leave his land and his country, his parents and patrimony" and go on pilgrimage. In this famous legend of Brendan's voyages we find adventures comparable to those of Ulysses as well as the presence of two great Irish soul friends who are women: Ita and Brigid. Ita, Brendan's foster-mother and spiritual guide, advises him to learn from the saints of Ireland about holiness and tells him that God is calling him to cross the seas in order "to instruct the souls of men." Without her presence in his life, Brendan might never have accomplished all that he yearned to see and do.

In *A Life of Maedoc of Ferne* we find how a relationship with one's *anamchara* appears to be more or less permanent:

> Another time Maedoc and an immature child were by a
> cross which there was in the monastery of Ferne. The child
> saw him mount a golden ladder which reached from earth
> to heaven; and when he descended later, the child could not
> look in his face for the great brilliance and resplendence of
> the Deity which transfused and beautified his countenance.

When asked by the child where he had gone, Maedoc replies:

> "I went," said he, "with the gladness of the company of
> heaven, to meet the soul of Columcille as it went to join
> them, who was my own soul friend in this world."

What is so powerful about this story is that it draws upon the
ladder imagery, a symbol and theme of spiritual progress persist-
ent in Judeo-Christian spirituality—from the dream of Jacob (Gn
28:12) to Jesus' own allusion to it (Jn 1:51), on through the writings of Origen, John Climacus, Walter Hilton, Luther, Calvin and
others. Thus, not only does this story of Maedoc seem to say that
soul friend relationships survive even death, but that soul friends
are a way toward union with God.

In the *Life of Bairre of Cork* we find an affirmation of a pattern
found among the desert fathers and mothers: Although a person
may have different spiritual guides in his or her life, the ultimate
anamchara or guide is God. After the death of an older monk who
had been his tutor, Bairre is "much concerned" about being without a soul friend and goes to visit Eolang, the head of another mon-
astery. Before Bairre can ask Eolang about being a soul friend,
Eolang kneels before him, and says:

> "I offer to thee my church, my body, and my soul." Then
> Bairre wept, and said: "This was not my thought, but that it
> would be I that would offer my church to thee." Eolang
> said: "Let it be as I say that it shall be; for this is the will of
> God. And thou are dear to God."

Then Eolang tells Bairre, "You will receive a soul friend worthy
of you at my hand today," and, according to the story, "this was
fulfilled: for Eolang placed Bairre's hand in the hand of the Lord
Himself; and he said: 'O Lord, take to thee this just man.' "

Other stories reveal still other patterns regarding the Irish soul
friend, but this last story about God as our ultimate soul friend reveals perhaps the most important lesson of all. It is one we quickly
forget when we are trying too hard, as mentors or spiritual mentors, to help someone change his or her life.

Attributes of a Contemporary Soul Friend

Looking back at the soul friend's origins, the practice of confession/guidance common to early Christian communities, the contributions of so many talented individuals in dry, wilderness areas and lush, green lands enables us to discover a link with a current phenomenon: the increasing interest in a relationship of depth, which often seems to be offered only by the psychiatric and counseling professions. Many Christians are now searching for a relationship that unites those professions' helpful insights and healing skills with the rich heritage of Judeo-Christian spirituality. While some seek a soul friend who is specially trained and has professional competence, others wonder whether they stand in that ancient tradition of spiritual mentoring. Are there some characteristics that can help identify a contemporary soul friend?

I believe that there are seven attributes that can be of help in this process of discernment. Like Thomas Merton, I presuppose that the foundation on which all of them are built is first of all "a normal, spontaneous human relationship in an atmosphere of pleasant and easy familiarity." If that is present at the outset, the following attributes will have a good possibility of growth.

First, a soul friend should possess the important characteristic of maturity. In Elie Wiesel's book *Night* the young Jewish son asks his father to find him a master to guide him in his study of mysticism. His father tells him that only at the age of 30 does one have the right to venture into that "perilous" world. "You must first study the basic subjects within your own understanding," he says. So also the more professional spiritual mentor: He or she can have all the talents and book knowledge while still a young person, but there is a wisdom that only comes with age, with facing one's own questions, crises and suffering. Age definitely does not guarantee maturity or wisdom, but it can help a great deal.

A second characteristic, often arising from the first, and certainly one of utmost importance, is that of compassion: the ability to hear what another is attempting to put into words, the ability to understand without judging, the ability to be with another in pain.

Third, genuine respect for others, their stories, their times of anguish and of joy is important. This respect begins with reflection upon one's own story, so that reasons for gratitude and praise can be discovered there. If a person has no sense of his or her history as a sacred journey, it is difficult to imagine how that person can help others discern the sacredness of theirs.

A fourth characteristic is the ability to keep things confidential, a form of respect for what has been disclosed and for the very real need we all have for privacy. Confidentiality builds trust and is expected of any professional counselor or guide in our society. It certainly can be expected of the spiritual guide.

A fifth characteristic is self-disclosure, the willingness to share parts of one's own journey when and where appropriate. If one presupposes that the soul friend speaks of a relationship characterized by mutuality, reciprocity, equality and rapport, it necessarily follows that encounters with this friend are not monologues. To be a soul friend includes the willingness to be honest and not hide behind what Jung would call a smoke-screen of professional, fatherly authority. This willingness to share also helps the other feel more comfortable in disclosing personal aspects. Any sacred journey is a journey shared.

A sixth characteristic of the soul friend is his or her need to be something of a scholar, one who is continually reflecting on personal questions and experiences in relationship with God. This faith seeking understanding—St. Anselm's definition of theology—presupposes a knowledge of Christian traditions, of scripture, of the culture in which one lives. To read the signs of the times, as Pope John XXIII advised, a person also must have some knowledge of psychology. This knowledge of and dialogue with psychology and psychiatry involve a critical stance as well as an appreciation of how psychology and theology can help each other understand the many-faceted dimensions of this mystery we call humankind.

Finally, a seventh characteristic, one that has been emphasized throughout our own Christian tradition, is the ability to discern the movements of the spirit in the heart. This gift is an attribute that has been equated with the image of ''physician of souls,'' someone with the ability and training to diagnose spiritual disease as well as to make recommendations for spiritual wholeness and health. Today, however, this image is subject to possible misinterpretation or contradiction, especially for those who have had less than satisfactory relationships with doctors. An image that may speak much more of the reciprocity and mutuality expected of the soul friend is that of midwife, a person intimately involved in the process of helping another bring something to birth; the doctor may be perceived as too clinical, too distantly involved. Whether doctor or midwife, the soul friend who acts in a professional capacity needs to have some form of training that emphasizes learning to listen to and identify the movements of the heart.

All of these characteristics are rooted ultimately in the individual soul friend's spirituality—his or her relationship to self, to others, to God. This spirituality necessarily includes an appreciation of one's own history and that of one's religious heritage; it presupposes the ongoing discernment of one's own vocation; it can be helped, as St. Patrick's story shows us, by paying attention to our dreams. It also includes a commitment to a process of ongoing conversion-reconciliation in one's own life. We will be looking at all of these aspects of spirituality and concerns of spiritual mentoring in the next two chapters, as well as discussing specific ways of developing them.

It is important, however, to remember that there is no one person who embodies all of the characteristics of a soul friend perfectly. We are, after all, human beings, not gods or goddesses. Like William James, I also presuppose that just as there are varieties of religious experience, so also there are varieties of spiritual mentors. Each one will have his or her unique story, will combine certain gifts and qualities and forms of guidance in a unique way, will attract those who might not feel at ease with someone else.

This phenomenon is beautifully described in *The Glass Bead Game*, a fictional work by Hermann Hesse. In a chapter called "The Father Confessor" he tells of two early desert fathers involved in a ministry of soul friendship, yet each very different from the other. Their different personalities result in different approaches to ministry. The first, Josephus, is described as "an ear," one who knows how to listen to the penitent, "to open his ears and his heart, to gather the man's sufferings and anxieties into himself and hold them, so that the penitent was sent away emptied and calmed.''

> He [Josephus] seemed to pass no judgment upon them and to feel neither pity nor contempt for the person confessing. Nevertheless, or perhaps for that very reason, whatever was confessed to him seemed not to be spoken into the void, but to be transformed, alleviated, and redeemed in the telling and being heard. Only rarely did he reply with a warning or admonition.

The other confessor, older than Josephus, is Father Dion, ''celebrated,'' as the story tells us, ''for being able to read the souls of those who sought him,'' a man who ''often surprised a faltering penitent by charging him bluntly with his still unconfessed sins.'' Dion was ''a great judge, chastiser, and rectifier''—not afraid to assign penances, castigations and pilgrimages nor of ordering people to marry or compelling enemies to make up. As Hesse so subtly says, Father Dion ''enjoyed the authority of a bishop.'' Two men of different backgrounds, ages and approaches to ministry, yet both effective in the care of souls, and both, as the story shows, eventually in need of each other for salvation.

There is no perfect way of being a soul friend. Ultimately one must look within one's heart and to the God who works through our strengths and weaknesses—most remarkably, it seems, and most often in spite of them. It is God who is our friend, our guide, our mentor, the one who loved us first. As Merton so wisely tells us, when it comes to spiritual guidance on our sacred journeys the soul friend or spiritual mentor ''is not to be regarded as a magical machine solving cases and declaring the will of God;'' he or she, rather, ''helps to strengthen us in our groping efforts to correspond with the grace of the Holy Spirit, who alone is the true Director in the fullest sense of the word.''

We come back once more to a primary concern of our Judeo-Christian spirituality: the development of a relationship of intimacy with God. Ireland is a land of Christian faith and spirituality, the land of Patrick, Brigid, Brendan, Ita and so many other saints and mentors, some long forgotten. Living on a beautiful island, the Irish have a tremendous appreciation of natural beauty and what that beauty has given them: a sense of awe, gratitude and a genuine respect for a power greater than themselves. Their tragic history has also made its contribution, helping them acknowledge their powerlessness and their need to reach out for help beyond themselves. In their long history relationships with soul friends have assisted many of them in doing so. Expressing themselves in song and poetry and stories shared, the Irish have found meaning in the stories of a wandering carpenter, preacher, healer and lover, who was called by many of the Irish, especially during the Middle Ages, their own true soul friend. Like them, Jesus appreciated the importance of family, of tribal identity, of a God whose power is present in human relationships and the gentleness of a breeze, in the love and forgiveness of a friend and the colors of a sunset playing on the ocean's depths.

Living in an age in which many thirst for vital connections and meaningful lives, a story from the Irish saint Moeog is worth telling:

> The inhabitants complained to Moeog that the place was waterless. "Dig at the root of yonder tree," said Moeog, "and you shall find a spring." They did so, and found as he said. And the stream began to flow.

If we take Moeog's advice and begin to dig at the roots of our spiritual traditions, we too might discover a refreshing spring, a flowing stream gathering in strength that comes to us from the source of living water (Jn 7:38).

FOUR

The Call of Life

His heart trembled in an ecstasy of fear and his soul was in
flight. This was the call of life to his soul not the dull gross
voice of the world of duties and despair. To live, to err, to
fall, to triumph, to recreate life out of life!

James Joyce, *A Portrait of the Artist as a Young Man*

In 1949, four years after the death of his father, Andrew
Wyeth painted a self-portrait called *The Revenant*. It depicts a
ghostlike man standing in a barren room with cracked walls, tattered shades and eerie lighting. The man appears to be returning
from a distant journey, now uncomfortable in the room he has just
re-entered after a long absence. The portrait represents Wyeth's
search for identity shortly after his father's accidental death. The
artist said the death left him feeling disoriented and disconnected
from everything. Painting the self-portrait was a way of beginning
to deal constructively with that sudden death. It was also a way of
expressing his own emerging sense of identity and vocation. "For
the first time in my life," he said, "I was painting with real reason
to do it."

I received a copy of the painting from a friend who later became my wife. It was my first Wyeth print, and although it meant a lot to me, I didn't really understand its meaning when I received it. Now I understand, because I see it with different eyes, with what the New England transcendentalist Ralph Waldo Emerson calls "a new angle of vision." I have changed since receiving that gift. I have experienced my own passage from exile to revenant. With the help of various mentors along the way I have discerned options, made choices and begun through my decisions to clarify my own identity and life-work. And yet Wyeth's self-portrait, which now hangs in our bedroom, reminds me that identity is never finished in this lifetime and that vocation is a *continuing* process of discerning who I am meant to be. Although I experience with my wife and sons a much greater sense of being at home and having a sense of purpose, my life—and my dreams—keep taking me into unfamiliar rooms with cracked walls, tattered shades and, at times, eerie lighting.

The Rediscovery of Vocation

In *Seasons of Strength* Evelyn and James Whitehead speak of a quiet revolution occurring in this country in which ancient distinctions between clergy and laity are giving way, and the time-honored separation between Christians who "have vocations" and those who don't is being bridged. According to the Whiteheads, a vocation refers to the sense that our lives are "for something," and although that intimation of purpose may at times be more murky than clear, many of us find ourselves with an inner drive "to be somebody" (as Martin Luther King so often preached), to do something with our lives. Psychologist Daniel Levinson tells us that a vocation is inextricably linked with a person's "dream:" that vision of the future that includes the kind of life and person we want to be, as well as our own personal myth in which we are the would-be heroes or heroines "engaged in a noble quest." It is this vision and myth associated with identity that often influence the choices and decisions we make and the direction our lives take—whether we are consciously aware of it or not. Levinson also believes that the most important role for any mentor is helping another person clarify that dream and bring it into actuality.

The word *vocation* itself comes from the Latin *vocare*, which means "to call." That sense of calling, or, as some people experience it, of being sent or led or even pulled or pushed is often associated with the transcendent, the holy, the Holy One, God. It begins when a person is quite young and can increase steadily, as a person grows older, into a profound hunger for fulfillment. This search for the transcendent so closely intertwined with the quest for meaning and identity during adulthood is universal, going beyond religious differences or denominational distinctions. Augustine described it in terms of the heart: "Our hearts are restless till they rest in thee, O Lord." Abraham Heschel, a modern Jewish writer, equated this search for ultimate meaning with "the great yearning that sweeps eternity: the yearning to praise, the yearning to serve." The Irish author James Joyce poetically referred to vocation as the call of life to the soul. However vocation is understood, the *experience* is often one of our being called. The deepest part of ourselves, our souls, are called through the outer events and people of our lives, as well as through our inner daemons or urgings, which, quite literally at times, will not leave us alone. It is a calling to become who we are meant to be, even though the outlines of that identity may seem extremely unclear and indistinct at times, like Wyeth's painting.

For the Christian the questions related to identity and meaning are intimately connected to two others as well: first, Whose am I? and second, Who am I called to serve? Because of our baptism and our own ongoing identification with Jesus' life and ministry, death and resurrection, we have been given a direction in which to search, a community to support our quest for answers, a God already revealed as companion on our sacred journeys through time. Even though we can never self-righteously presuppose that questions of vocation have been answered once and for all, we can experience moments of affirmation when particularly difficult decisions have been made and a sense of purpose has been articulated. Friends and mentors are often those who help us clarify the options and, after leaving us alone to make the choices, affirm the direction we have chosen. They can also lovingly challenge us to fulfill our potentials when they perceive that we are not. If we look to other lives for some greater clarification of the meaning of vocation, we find a great variety of ways that vocation is discovered and a great variety of responses to that discovery.

Varieties of Vocational Discovery and Response

Sometimes a sense of calling comes to us through our reading of scripture and reflection upon it—as it did for Augustine when, before his conversion, he heard the voice of a child in a garden telling him to "take up and read." Sometimes it may come to us in a dream, as it did for the great missionary to the Irish, Patrick. Sometimes the sense of vocation comes through an experience of long loneliness, as described by the Catholic activist Dorothy Day in an autobiography of that name. At times we recognize the calling, as did the Lutheran theologian Reinhold Niebuhr, in our discernment of social injustices and our need to respond in some way. Sometimes, like the Trappist monk Thomas Merton, our hunger for ideas, convictions and meaning lead us to an ever-deepening desire to give ourselves totally to God in some explicit way. Sometimes we only discover our true vocation after years of searching and many career changes as Anton Boisen, the father of clinical pastoral education, describes in his autobiography, *Out of the Depths*. The Anglican spiritual writer Evelyn Underhill found hers only after experiencing a breakdown in her 40s.

As the recognition of a vocation comes to us in differing ways, so also can our responses to that discernment process vary greatly. For certain people such a discovery is an exhilarating and sometimes totally unforeseen experience. Russell Baker, for example, in his autobiography, *Growing Up*, tells us of the feeling of ecstasy when his essay on "The Art of Eating Spaghetti" was unexpectedly read aloud by his teacher to his classmates:

> My words! He was reading my words out loud to the entire class. What's more, the entire class was listening. Listening attentively. Then somebody laughed, then the entire class was laughing, not in contempt and ridicule, but with openhearted enjoyment. . . . I did my best to avoid showing

pleasure, but what I was feeling was pure ecstasy at this startling demonstration that my words had the power to make people laugh. In the eleventh grade, at the eleventh hour as it were, I had discovered a calling. It was the happiest moment of my entire school career. . . . For the first time, light shone on a possibility!

The discovery of his vocation to be a writer was obviously a happy one in which the teacher as mentor and his class of peers and their response of laughter contributed a great deal.

For others, the discovery of a vocation is associated with a great deal of ambivalence, especially when it comes in the loneliness of discerning who we are *not* meant to be. In James Joyce's *A Portrait of the Artist as a Young Man* Stephen Dedalus is asked a question by a Jesuit priest, his spiritual mentor at a boys' school, "Have you ever felt that you had a vocation [to the priesthood]?" The question at first disturbs and then haunts Stephen, but it also eventually helps him clarify that, although he is not meant to be a priest, he does have a vocation that lies somewhere else. In a statement reflecting his own life story Joyce writes about the young man:

He [Stephen] would never swing the thurible before the tabernacle as a priest. His destiny was to be elusive of social or religious orders. . . . He was destined to learn his own wisdom apart from others or to learn the wisdom of others himself wandering among the snares of the world.

With this affirmation of who he was *and of who he was not*, Stephen's "heart trembled; his breath came faster and a wild spirit passed over his limbs as though he were soaring sunward. His heart trembled in an ecstasy of fear and his soul was in flight." For the young artist, the discovery of his vocation, "the call of life to his soul," was an experience both frightening and filled with joy.

Other people equate their discovery of call with an experience of struggle and sometimes great reluctance to accept the call when it is presented as a choice. Dorothy Day, before her conversion to Roman Catholicism, was living with a man whom she loved very much, Forster, but who was opposed to any affiliation with a church. She tells us in *The Long Loneliness* that ''it was impossible to talk about religion or faith to him. A wall immediately separated us.'' When she became pregnant with his child, she knew that she must make a choice between Forster's love and her love for God and the child:

> I knew that I was going to have my child baptized, cost what it may. I knew that I was not going to have her floundering through many years as I had done, doubting and hesitating, undisciplined and amoral. I felt it was the greatest thing I could do for my child. For myself, I prayed for the gift of faith. I was sure, yet not sure. I postponed the day of decision. . . . Becoming a Catholic would mean facing life alone and I clung to family life. . . . So I waited.

Very reluctantly, she eventually realized that her conversion, so intimately linked to her understanding of her identity as a Christian and her vocation of motherhood, needed to be expressed publicly. She was right, however, about Forster's reaction, and she courageously accepted the long loneliness of life without him.

There are many ways we may begin to experience a sense of vocation in our lives—surely as many ways as there are people who experience that call of life. Perhaps the call itself is never recognized as decisively or as clearly as it seems to be by those who later write of their discovery. What many of us may have in common, however, is what Socrates called a ''kind of inner voice'' that cannot be stilled, or an emerging inner conviction, articulated by John Henry Newman, that refuses to be silenced: ''God has created me to do him some definite service; he has committed some work to me.'' This inner conviction or voice is, for many, eventually perceived as the voice of God, a moment of grace, contact with the sacred, the call of life to our souls. Based upon our experiences, most of us would probably agree that our response to this call is more often one of reluctance, like Dorothy Day's, or of some ambivalence, like Stephen's. Again, many of us could describe how often that call has transcended our conscious expectations, as well as interrupted, or seemed to interrupt, the ''certain'' direction in which we were headed. Others of us, as we grow older and hopefully wiser, could acknowledge our surprise at discovering that vocation itself is a life-long process of discernment, of listening to our deepest self, often with the help of mentors and friends. There is certainly no simple once-in-a-lifetime decision made upon reaching adulthood that finds a safe niche from which we can watch the rest of the world go by. The discovery of our vocation, however, the discernment of our Dream, the desire to be somebody who contributes to other lives—those experiences are often linked to experiences of conversion in our lives.

Today's Flowering of New Ministries

It is obvious among both lay people and ordained that our understanding and perception of the meaning of vocation is in transition. As in the early Irish church with its wide creativity in spirituality and inclusiveness in ministry, we are beginning to experience a flowering of ministries, a rich diversity of gifts and talents, which are only recently being recognized and shared. This flowering finds its roots in a new awareness among people that they do, in fact, have something to contribute and that, as church, they have the responsibility to do so. This flowering also finds its origins in individual and communal experiences of conversion. There is the growing realization that not only has God spoken to the prophets of old, the apostles who knew Jesus, the saints of other cultures and centuries, but that God is continuing to reveal his love and forgiveness, her wisdom and creativity to each of us. In the midst of good times and bad, our relationships with spouse, children, relatives and peers, which so often disturb our lives and so consistently amaze us, we are beginning to see God's presence and loving power. Experiences of birth, marital conflict, friendship with parents, the painful aging and death of our grandparents, celebrations of anniversaries, encounters with unexpected and unexplainable suffering—all raise questions seeking clarification and response. Sometimes joyfully, at times ambivalently, more often than not reluctantly, many of us have come to see that we are on a journey through time—one that needs to be shared if it is to be experienced as worthwhile. To perceive our journeys as sacred journeys, to discern our vocations, which like tapestries continue to unfold in length and color and sometimes awesome beauty, depends upon our acknowledging that sacred dimension to our lives and expressing it in stories told in word and deed, ritual and ministry.

To see our lives as sacred journeys is a theme we find expressed repeatedly in our rich Judeo-Christian heritage—from the Exodus journey of the Israelites with its trials and eventual liberation to Jesus' journey to Jerusalem, which brought suffering *and* salvation. It is a theme expressed too in allegorical form from John Bunyan's *Pilgrim's Progress* to C. S. Lewis' *Pilgrim's Regress*. We also find it in the documents of Vatican II, identifying Christians as a "pilgrim people" who, as church, are on the move toward the Promised Land through sometimes dry and parched wildernesses. Some of us can identify the moment when that theme and that tradition became a living reality for us, when we stopped considering the sacred only in terms of other people's lives and began to see our sacred memories and moments as worthy of dialogue with theirs. Many of us cannot precisely identify when this realization happened, but are aware that some gradual process of awakening resulted in a new awareness, a more adult recognition of God as a caring, higher power worthy of our trust. Whenever and however that sense, intuition, conviction enters our lives, a turning point is reached, conversion happens, transformation begins.

Sometimes age has something to do with it—the questions of emerging adulthood or the onslaught of mid-life or the growing realization of our own mortality. Often conversion begins with a specific encounter in which significant questions of meaning are raised or with especially disturbing experiences of disorientation and powerlessness. Recovering people speak about hitting bottom, the stark conviction that one's life cannot go on as it has. Others describe how an unexpected illness, the loss of a job, the move to another city or country, the failure of a marriage, or even the attainment of life's goals have led to an encounter with God. C. S. Lewis, as we have seen, describes how darkness within, "a zoo of lusts, a bedlam of ambitions, a nursery of fears, a harem of fondled hatreds," helped him recognize the need for change. Significant experiences of transformation, however, do not have to be associated only with crises and suffering. The birth of Dorothy Day's baby, Tamar, for example, was a spiritual experience of great joy revealing God's love and giving her the courage to change her life. Bede Griffiths, Lewis' student, also tells us that the conversion process can be initiated with an experience of unexpected awe:

> One day during my last term at school I walked out alone in the evening and heard the birds singing in that full chorus of song which can only be heard at that time of year at dawn or at sunset. I remember now the shock of the surprise with which the sound broke on my ears. It seemed to me that I have never heard the birds singing before and I wondered whether they sang like this all the year round and I had never noticed it. As I walked on I came upon some hawthorn trees in full bloom and again I thought that I had never seen such a sight or experienced such sweetness before. . . . A lark rose suddenly from the ground beside the tree where I was standing and poured out its song above my head. Everything then grew still as the sunset faded and the veil of dusk began to cover the earth. I remember now the feeling of awe which came over me. I felt inclined to kneel on the ground, as though I had been standing in the presence of an angel; and I hardly dared to look on the face of the sky, because it seemed as though it was but a veil before the face of God.

In retrospect, Bede saw his experience as one of the decisive moments of his life, one that revealed to him the sacramental character of all of nature and the presence of a loving God. "Suddenly we know," he writes in *The Golden String*, "that we belong to another world, that there is another dimension to existence." The experience eventually led him to the conversion called Christian, in which the God he experienced in nature is identified with a particular human-divine story and a particular spirituality.

In the writings of the lay theologian Rosemary Haughton we find one of the best descriptions of conversion because it is rooted in experiences that so many of us have. A convert to Roman Catholicism, mother of a large family now grown, and presently ministering to abused and homeless women in Gloucester, Massachusetts, at Wellspring House, she is a pastoral theologian with a great deal of wisdom. Let us turn to her for a better understanding of what the process of conversion entails.

Stages of Transformation

In Haughton's book *The Transformation of Man* conversion or "transformation" is defined as a "total revolution, a complete change of the mode of existence from the estrangement and muddle of sin to sharing in the life of God." Though it may be identified as occurring in a sudden and dramatic event, it nevertheless comes as the culmination of a long process and continues on as a life-long process in which people struggle to live a life of real love. In Haughton's numerous works she draws upon many examples from ordinary human experience as well as from literature, plays and poetry to express her theology of conversion and community. She believes that transformation leads to "the birth of the whole human being" and to reconciliation and communion, "a sharing in a new community of life."

Positing that we are born into a state of "enclosure and ignorance" (that is, limited by our physical bodies in what we can do and what we know), our only way of breaking out is through the activity of love. Formation, which Haughton defines as "education for loving," is concerned with creating patterns of behavior for our children that teach them—and us—about the importance of unselfishness, self-discipline, courtesy and good manners. This education or formation, however, is not what she means by transformation. The difference between the two, Haughton says, is analogous to the difference between behavior that is imposed and imitative, and behavior that springs from the authentic self. Though formation is a necessary process, it only creates the possibility of a spiritual breakthrough or personal revolution; it does not guarantee that it will happen. In fact, Haughton believes that genuine transformation is only realized when formation breaks down.

Transformation, according to her, finds its opportunity precisely in those places and stages in life when the personality lacks a supporting framework, when our lives are the most confused and disorganized. Such opportunities occur at times of emotional upheaval, crisis and suffering. It can also happen with the impact of sexual passion in adult life. As disorienting and painful as such times can be, making our lives seem out of control, producing violence, resentment, hatred and even despair, they can also be opportunities the spirit needs in order to break down barriers of self-delusion and sin. Haughton associates sin with the recognition that we not only have committed harmful and destructive acts, but that we live in a sinful state that is "not simply a state suffered, but *my* responsibility." This awareness and the acceptance of responsibility for it she calls repentance or conversion.

Haughton clearly believes that the human experiences that can lead to transformation are always dependent upon relationships of love. From a Christian perspective they are also implicitly connected with Christ, whom she calls the image and representative of "the authentic human spirit." Preceded by the process of formation, in which the most important part is the experience of being loved, transformation itself follows the pattern of many conversions, beginning in what Haughton calls "the wilderness," the in-between state when the structures of formation have broken down and only the choice to love or not to love remains. She associates this wilderness state with experiences of conflict, crisis and estrangement, where "something happens that makes the normal structure of security . . . seem no longer safe or even very real," where "there is a loss of self-respect, a loss of a feeling of belonging to anything." It is that time, produced by what Haughton describes as "an encounter," that can act as an impetus to change our lives and lead us ultimately to communion and reconciliation with God and others in a genuinely new way. What emerges in Haughton's writings is a pattern of conversion-reconciliation consisting of the following elements, stages or series of events, not necessarily distinct, but often overlapping:

1. *Encounter:* An encounter occurs when people meet and react to each other in startling and unpredictable ways, producing in a totally unplanned manner the wilderness experience or in-between

state described above. Such encounters, whether between two
children who quarrel, for example, or between a man and woman
who experience the power of passion for the first time, can lead to
a decision where one either responds lovingly or refuses to love. If
one chooses to love, transformation happens in that moment of
self-surrender, and, as such, is seen by Haughton as an act of faith,
a total abandonment, a jump into the void, a response of love that
is set against an unknowable future. Such a response is made possible when one has the knowledge of being loved already. Although it may be very painful at times, since it can involve a dying
to self, surrender of ourselves in love has the possibility of creating new life, one that is shared.

2. *Self-discovery:* An encounter and the decision to love can
create a new relationship between people as well as a new awareness, paradoxically, of the messy human condition in which we
live and the unloving behavior in which we often indulge. This
new knowledge of self as loved *and* sinful can lead to a turning-
away from all that prevents the self-giving of love, a reordering
and replanning of one's life. This experience, for the Christian, is
named repentance. Again, what often leads to the desire to repent
or change our lives, according to Haughton, is the experience of
our being loved *first.* Because I am loved by someone, when I discover the wonder of this reality I naturally want to be more
lovable—to engage in more loving behavior. This is true of adults
as well as of children, of anyone, whatever the age; it applies in
our relationships with one another and with God. Somehow the
discovery that I am loved, for any of us, gives us a new identity and
new ability to change our selfish, self-destructive ways.

3. *Release of Power:* Through self-discovery and repentance
new power is released in the lives of people. This power leads to
reconciliation, healing, harmony, peace. Such power changes a
person, like the Old Testament prophets, into what Haughton calls
an "agent of transformation":

> The power that is released when a person is seized with the
> spirit of prophesy is the same power that works in the little,
> unnoticed prophetic utterances by which human beings

bring salvation to each other. . . . This prophetic sending is
a mission on which every person is sent to every other person, and this "sending" is itself the intervention that can
shape the outbreak of power in another.

Experiencing the power of love in our lives can lead us all to
become active as agents of change in our society and church, with
our families and friends. We come to lovingly challenge institutions that are causing people to suffer for the wrong reasons; we
intervene gently but firmly when we see others bent on self-
destructive and sometimes suicidal behavior; most of all, we invite
others to a possibly healthier and more spiritually enriching way of
life, perhaps not so much through our words, but through our very
real, concrete, loving deeds. With the experience of "release of
power," we are naturally led to Haughton's fourth stage.

4. *Community:* The outbreak of power that transforms one into
an agent of transformation creates community. It transforms the
individual, converting him or her out of the formation community,
which prepared the person through its loving relationships, and
into the converted community, which he or she must build. For the
Christian such a community is called church, and it is this "on-
purpose" community—in the Spirit—that is meant to be for others, according to Haughton, "Christ poor, Christ serving, Christ
healing." The task of the church as "the-people-who-know-they-
are-the-church" is to provide formation suited to transformation,
to create transforming opportunities for our children—and
ourselves—with the realization that transformation is always
something that happens outside of our own efforts. As Haughton
subtly warns us, "nobody can lay it on to order."

Haughton illustrates through many examples in her writings
that the conversion or transformation process—which ultimately
leads to a change of identity, a realization of vocation and union
with God—is intimately related to the ordinary events and persons
of our lives. What emerges in all of these examples is her conviction that transformation is a common human occurrence dependent upon the power of love. Such transformation often leads to
participation in a new community and relationships of care that

continue to invite positive change in ourselves and the society and
church to which we belong.

There are many implications in Haughton's writings concerning the ministry of mentoring in general and spiritual mentoring in
particular. We have only to reflect on the experiences of being in
the wilderness in our own lives to recognize how important it is at
the "encounter" stage to have a loving friend or community of
friends to help us through it; we have only to realize, once we have
made the transition to "self-discovery" and "release of power,"
how much that new sense of identity and meaning comes as a result
of some person, friend or mentor having loved us *first*. For those
of us who now identify ourselves as church, we often discover
upon reflection that our ministries and involvement in society and
church are the direct result of people having mentored us without
our even being aware of their transforming presence in our lives.

However we discover the reality of our being loved and the
reality of God—whether through experiences of inner darkness
described by Lewis, or an aesthetic experience discussed by Griffiths, or those wilderness experiences described by Haughton—
we are changed profoundly and our histories are divided between
before and after that change.

Ministry and the Discernment of Our Call

For many people experiences of transformation at different
stages of life and involving various vocational decisions can lead
them to the recognition of a call to ministry. As the co-founder of
Alcoholics Anonymous, Bill Wilson, expressed it, "Life gives us
moments; for those moments we give our lives." When we have
experienced positive growth in ourselves and recognized that we
have been given certain gifts, we naturally want to share our talents and competence with others. This is often the motivation behind the ministry of mentoring: coming to a realization of the
many ways in which we have been mentored, we want to mentor
others in return in whatever ways we can.

Whatever form of ministry we become involved in as a result
of a conversion process, we discover that ministry in its broadest
sense is not something we put on like a collar; ministry emerges

out of those patterns of our lives that reveal gifts received and a desire to return them with gratitude. Whether or not we decide to have them recognized in some official way or put to use in a setting specifically identified as church, our ministries always need to be rooted in a grateful appreciation of gifts received and a healthy awareness of our own limitations. They also need, besides the very important inner affirmation that we have something to contribute, an outer affirmation, a discernment by others on the grassroots level of our daily lives and work that those gifts and the desire to serve are genuine.

Ministry begins with our personal relationships of family, friends, colleagues and mentors. It is their discernment process, expressed to us when they might say, "You know, you're really good at that" or "People come to you because you listen so well," that is crucial to our own discovery of vocation and of discerning options and making choices regarding what ministries we can and should do. No matter how many ceremonies of laying on of hands or how many good intentions we might have, effective ministry will not happen unless those close to us have also guided us with their insight and their wisdom.

According to spiritual writer Alan Jones in *Exploring Spiritual Direction*, "the gift is recognized through the slow process of persons seeking him or her out for counsel or advice." Often the person they seek is puzzled, wondering "why are these people coming to me?" It is then that such a person needs to be informed about the long and rich tradition of spiritual guidance, Jones says, and "begin to learn about those who have preceded him or her." Being in touch with this tradition and some of the wisdom figures in its long line can be a great comfort. That is why specific theology and spirituality courses, as well as the reading of our Judeo-Christian great books can often help. Jones also says that knowing that such a vocation is not our decision alone, and that others can assist us in its discernment, can alleviate some of our anxiety about whether we're called to be spiritual mentors. While our deepest selves, including the warts as well as the gifts, are involved here, it is not the self alone, according to Jones, but the self "enlivened by the Holy Spirit" that chooses to go into the ministry of spiritual guidance. The list of characteristics associated in the preceding chapter on the soul friend tradition could also help a person discern whether he or she is called to this form of ministry.

Still, disturbing questions and doubts about ourselves and our participation in ministry—whether in church or marketplace settings—can persist. More aware of God's goodness and presence in our lives as a result of some conversion experience, we sometimes wonder how to translate emerging convictions into specific actions or ministries. Living in a church that has inherited traditions from the past for good and for ill, many of us are aware of the need for ongoing structural reforms that will invite more people to participate in ministry and the "on-purpose community" that Haughton describes. Some of us, as career ministers, lay and ordained, are struggling not only to encourage the ministries of all, but to find ways to protect ourselves from burn-out and the ravages of other forms of emotional suicide. If we are Roman Catholics, we are part of a church in transition, attempting at times to incorporate and at other times resist the revolutionary vision of Vatican II. As a result we may feel as do the characters in Charles Dickens' *Tale of Two Cities*, the story of another revolution and of the people caught in it, that we are experiencing the best of times and the worst of times, that we are living in an age of wisdom and of foolishness, a season of light and darkness, a springtime of hope and a winter of despair. These ambivalent feelings and the questions that accompany them need not and should not be repressed, for they are sources of more learning and of more self-awareness, the foundation of any and all ministry. They also offer the church as an institution, and each of us as members, the opportunity for clarifying vocations still emerging, dreams unspoken, ministries yet to be enfleshed. As the poet Rilke advises, we need patience with the questions themselves, which often seem like "locked rooms and like books that are written in a foreign language"; we need to live the questions now so that we might gradually "live along some distant day into the answer." Attempting to answer these profoundly sacred questions can lead us in unexpected directions along uncharted and often very painful paths. But, hopefully, because of previous and present experiences of friendship and love, we will be able to continue. Such questions and times of uncertainty can make us especially aware of the need for someone else to guide us in our ongoing search for identity, meaning and, ultimately, since vocational questions are so important, salvation. Like the young Jewish boy, Eleizer, in Elie Wiesel's book *Night*, already mentioned, we may begin to see the need for a spiritual mentor to help us discern where and to whom we are being called. Perhaps such a friendly guide as Eleizer's Moche the Beadle may even affirm for us the value of the questions being asked. "Every question," he tells the boy, "possesses a power that does not necessarily lie in the answer." We raise ourselves toward God by the questions we ask of him:

> That is the true dialogue. Man questions God and God answers. . . . You will find the true answers, Eleizer, only within yourself! . . . There are a thousand and one gates leading into the orchard of mystical truth. Every human being has his own gate. We must never make the mistake of wanting to enter the orchard by any gate but our own.

All of us have our own way of living out the truth of our lives as we discern that truth and attempt to live by it. Though we might like to be, and sometimes quite unconsciously attempt to be another Augustine, Patrick, Lewis, Day, Niebuhr, Boisen, Underhill, Newman or even Jesus, we cannot be them. We can, however, live our lives and our vocations as authentically as they did theirs, by responding courageously to the questions of our lives and times, to the vivid outer experiences and inner voices that keep pursuing us.

How to Discern Our Call

If we agree with Daniel Levinson that the most essential function of mentoring is to support and help someone else clarify his or her dream, and, as we learned from the life of C.S. Lewis, that such mentoring becomes an important form of empowerment, then we can see that helping others discern their vocations, name their talents and begin to give shape to their dreams is a tremendous ministry. We know this from those who helped us at certain times of our lives. Without the love of certain significant mentors, we would not be the same today.

How can we help others become empowered for ministry, more accepting of their gifts and talents as they clarify the call of life to their souls? Obviously, there is no quick or easy answer, but sometimes this important aspect of mentoring can be initiated with a simple question or series of questions: What is your dream? your ambition? the direction you would like to see your life take? The beauty of James Joyce's *Portrait of the Artist as a Young Man* and Elie Wiesel's *Night* is that the mentors in each initiated the questions about vocation and affirmed whatever answers those whom they were mentoring discovered for themselves. As a teacher and mentor to others over the years, I am increasingly aware that many people have never been asked such questions or been encouraged to define their dream *for themselves*. Whether we are in need of mentoring or are a spiritual mentor for someone else, let us consider how we can begin to listen, to take seriously the questions of our identities and the possible directions of our lives. How can we discern our call when we have been awakened by some form of crisis or conversion that has left its mark and affected our spirituality?

Presupposing that the discernment of vocation is an ongoing process, I recommend that we begin with the attempt to tell our own stories, identifying them for ourselves.

In the 1800s, my great-great-grandfather Martin Foy came to Minnesota from Ireland. He took up farming in southern Minnesota, near New Ulm, and retired in 1890 to Springfield. There he wrote an autobiography entitled *Trials and Experience of Frontier Life on the Western Prairie*. In it, he states that ''every man and woman has a story to tell; many of them have a story to tell much like my own.'' I have come to appreciate his wisdom, for it seems to me that no matter who we are and no matter how eloquent or otherwise, if we tell our own story with some degree of honesty and concreteness, it will be an interesting story and, if related in a personal way, it will be in some sense a universal story. Attempting to name the good times and bad, the significant people who have influenced us—for better or worse—is a way of contemplation, a way of seeking wisdom, a way of prayer. When we take time to look back over our lives for certain themes and patterns (ones that are easy to miss when we are caught up in the process of living them) we are affirming that our stories are, in fact, sacred journeys; that possibly within them we can find the seeds of our ministries and intimations of our calls. A person does not have to be a great writer, merely a person who wants to discover the truth of his or her life, a truth that begins to emerge as we reflect on our lives and times and begin to write down our stories.

To facilitate that writing, let us consider some questions that might help us focus on our past and on our future dreams, and thus help us discover who we are, whose we are, whom we are called to serve. Here are some categories with which to begin:

1. *Family Roots*: What was my relationship with my parents like? What was my relationship with my brothers and sisters like? What did I learn from them? What gifts did I receive from my family that I might contribute to other people's lives? What did family illnesses teach me about promoting better physical, psychological and spiritual health? What is my most painful memory from childhood? What is my happiest? What have these and other experiences of pain and joy taught me about myself, God and others whose lives I touch? What cultural heritage was passed on to me? What spirituality is mine because of this heritage?

2. *Significant Persons*: Are there certain people in my life besides my immediate family who taught me certain values, who formed me with their love? What mentors have befriended me and encouraged me to become more fully myself? When were they significant and why? What specific things about the importance of caring for others did I learn from them? To whom am I grateful and for what? From whom do I feel alienated and why? In what ways can I acknowledge my gratitude for gifts received or my own need for reconciliation?

3. *Significant Events*: Are there certain events, good times and bad, turning points, that have had an effect on my life? What were they, and in what way are they significant? What specific crises

have led me to a new understanding of God? In what ways have I experienced God's presence or absence? Are there certain changes I've made, geographic moves I've taken, or places I associate with a new awareness of myself?

4. *My Dream:* What is my dream—what kind of person do I want to be, and what kind of life do I want to live? What is the vision that motivates me? What do I want out of life? What do I want to give it? What do I perceive as my life work? Where would I like to be in five years? What would I like to be doing?

5. *Patterns:* Upon reflection, do any patterns in my life tell me something about the way I relate to others, myself and God? Do they reveal certain values I want to uphold? What patterns related to my behavior and feelings reveal a healthy spirituality or have led to self-destructive behavior in the past? Are there patterns that have brought some personal integrity, happiness and satisfaction into my life? Are there certain gifts that I can contribute to my family, society and church?

6. *A Title:* Titles of books often summarize what the book is really about. They help us focus the content of an entire work in a few words or a short phrase; for example, Dorothy Day's autobiography, *The Long Loneliness*, is about her loneliness without Forster and, because of it, her continuing search for community and intimacy with God. Thomas Merton's *Seven Storey Mountain* is a story of repentance and conversion, a "climb" to holiness and God. C. S. Lewis' *Surprised by Joy* is about a life journey initially in search of joy, which ultimately led him to an encounter with its Source. After reflecting on my story, what would I entitle it? Why?

Seeking Gifts to Share

These questions cannot be answered hurriedly. We need time for reflection, for listening and beginning to see the richness of our lives. We also need to begin our writing with modest expectations, not demanding that our story be so perfect or so dramatic as to be suitable material for a movie or play. (Many of us perhaps already believe that not even a novel or movie could adequately describe some aspects of our lives!) Rather, we write our life story for ourselves, as a way of beginning to appreciate the *whole* story and the gifts that might be in need of acknowledgement, gratitude and sharing. This writing of our story need not be the length of a book, but perhaps only a short chapter.

Those who simply cannot write for one reason or another can find alternatives. Some might prefer to keep an oral journal, for example, simply reflecting aloud into a tape recorder those memories of people and events that come to mind. Others may prefer to express their stories through drawing, painting or collecting old photographs. Whatever seems to fit, re-collecting our memories and continuing to reflect on our stories as they unfold can be a way of acknowledging them so that they can finally be claimed gratefully as our own, revealing our deeper selves, our souls.

Another way of discerning the mystery that surrounds us and the possible traces of a vocation found in our storytelling is that of journaling. In our journal we can begin to respond to the questions of our daily life and to the broader vocational questions of who we are becoming. Both *journal* and *journey* come from the French *le jour* meaning "day." Journaling can become a way of reflecting upon our daily journeys, as well as a way of preparing to write our life stories. It does not necessarily capture one day's or year's mystery, but can assist us in becoming more fully aware of the sacred mystery that is a part of every life and every day—and its Source.

There is no right or wrong method of journaling. What is important is that through effort and practice we discover *our* way. Anything that seems appropriate to the person doing the writing can be recorded in a journal, from an account of significant (or seemingly very insignificant) daily events and feelings associated with them to a description of dreams, the ones that come to us at night or those daydreams that haunt us in our waking hours. In the next chapter, we will discuss dreams and what they can teach us regarding the ongoing discernment of our vocations, as well as the greater awareness of self so essential to our spiritual mentoring.

Whatever the content of our journals, journaling can help clarify our present situation and give us a glimpse into the future as we reflect on who we are becoming. Journaling can also offer us the opportunity to examine the past where unhealed memories need to be named and reconciled. Whatever the focus, each of us needs to find a method that is meaningful to us, as well as a time and place where we can attain some solitude to write.

As a practice, journaling has been used by all sorts of people, from Ralph Waldo Emerson to Reinhold Niebuhr, Pope John XXIII to Dorothy Day, Dag Hammarskjold to Thomas Merton, F. Scott Fitzgerald to Virginia Woolf. Besides the increase of self-awareness that journaling brings—certainly an important attribute of anyone who ministers—there can gradually come an awareness that this journaling is a form of worship and a form of prayer. If we take seriously C. S. Lewis' analogy that contemplation is "the daughter of wisdom," we can appreciate how journaling is a way to wisdom itself. Keeping a journal or writing a life story, either can lead to sharing our reflections with family and friends, or with a spiritual mentor or soul friend. Out of such sharing we may eventually come to the understanding expressed by Thomas Merton in his autobiography, *The Seven Storey Mountain*, that all vocations, indeed all stories, are meant to reveal *one* vocation, *one* story whose origin is God:

> Whether you teach or live in the cloister or nurse the sick, whether you are in religion or out of it, married or single, no matter who you are or what you are, you are called . . . to a deep interior life, perhaps even to mystical prayer, and to pass the fruits of your contemplation on to others. And if you cannot do so by word, then by example.

In an obvious reference to his own sacred journey and discernment of vocation, Merton describes the experience of us all: "In one sense we are always travelling, and travelling as if we did not know where we were going. In another sense we have already arrived."

FIVE

Dream Figures:
Mentors of the Soul

Natural transformation processes announce themselves
mainly in dreams. . . . This "other being" [in the process
of inner transformation and rebirth] is the other person in
ourselves—that larger and greater personality maturing
within us, whom we have already met as the inner friend of
the soul.

Carl Jung, *Four Archetypes*

Carl Jung, a pioneer in dream analysis, once said that although
people call faith the true religious experience, they do not stop and
think that actually it is a secondary phenomenon. The real source
of faith, according to Jung, is that something happens to us in the
first place that instills trust and loyalty. This "something" can occur in a variety of ways, but one of special importance for Jung is
the mysterious language and symbols of our dreams. They can
contribute in a significant way, Jung thought, to our emotional and
spiritual maturation, and when we seek to discern their meaning a

103

Self is born, the larger and greater personality maturing within us, the person we are called to be.

Reflecting on my own life and the transitions I have made, I have come to appreciate the ideas of Jung. Time and again my dreams, as wise spiritual mentors, have pointed out new directions or creative tasks yet to be accomplished. Or, as healing agents, my dreams have forced me to acknowledge aspects of my life and personality that I persistently sought to ignore. For me, attempting to interpret and understand my dreams is part of my continuing process of discerning my vocation and increasing my self-awareness. With their diversity of characters and plots, dreams have been, and continue to be, encounters with a loving, compassionate God. They have also been topics of discussion each month with my own spiritual mentor, who does not *tell* me what they mean, but rather, through the right questions or comments, helps me discern for myself their meaning.

I don't recall any discussion or acknowledgement of the value of dreams in my childhood and adolescent years. My parents, teachers and mentors never referred to them until the time of my grandfather's death; a few days before, my mother cried at breakfast because of a dream she had had the previous night that his death was imminent. Only when I began graduate studies at the University of Notre Dame did my dreams become a source of learning and discerning the direction of my life. During a practicum experience under the supervision of a Lutheran pastor who became a soul friend to me, I was invited into the world of the unconscious, into the realm of shadows and of light.

During our first meeting I was describing the painful transition from being a teacher to being a student again when Fritz said to me, "I have the image of you on a seashore with one foot in the water and one foot in the sand." Then, he added, "Have you ever dreamed?" His simple question was the beginning of a process that is continuing to this day. Although I had rarely remembered my dreams, I began to do so much more consistently with his help. That first semester at Notre Dame became filled with dreams, and the more I shared them with Fritz, the more I seemed to remember.

There were dreams that I still recall. In fact, the first one I had after that opening session—when Fritz coached me on how to go about remembering dreams—seemed to be a microcosm of my life. Raised in a series of small towns in Minnesota and North Dakota, I find myself in this first dream once again in the country. I am walking along a country road and then enter a white, clapboard church where a funeral is about to begin. I approach the bier and, although I do not recognize the man, notice that he is an adult about my age. Quite unexpectedly, I also realize that he is naked, like a newborn or like a man stripped of everything. As I turn away I perceive that this supposedly dead man is very much alive and that he is rising slowly from the coffin! Amazed, I experience a great deal of ambivalence. I am afraid but also fascinated by this unusual phenomenon. At the same time I try to ignore his presence and all that is happening.

I awoke and later shared the dream with Fritz. Neither of us realized then how much it captured what would eventually occur as a result of my taking the unconscious seriously. It was the beginning for me of a difficult passage to a new self and identity in adulthood, which emerged from *my* interior values rather than someone else's expectations of who I should be.

Some of this transformation process, which began at Notre Dame, involved not only dealing honestly with present conflicts and future goals, but with unresolved issues from my past. The wisdom of the unconscious was manifest here, for no sooner had I dreamed of the funeral and living corpse than other dreams took me back to my childhood and my relationship with my parents. Evidently, the unconscious knew that primary relationships from those early years must first be acknowledged and reconciled before moving on to other areas and relationships. Once those had been named and discussed with Fritz, still other dreams appeared specifically related to my emerging vision of church and ministry.

As I continued my graduate studies, I became convinced that the reality of church was much broader than the one with which I had grown up, and that the church's ministries should include many more people than the relatively few ordained. My dreams reflected this growing recognition. The more I studied the rich and diverse history of Christian spirituality, the more I came to realize, supported by Vatican II, that the churches themselves must strive for reconciliation and greater unity.

There was one dream in particular that confirmed this emerging conviction. In it, I am standing with a guide, a Thomas Merton figure, overlooking white, circular buildings in a valley far below. Each building is connected by passageways, forming a mandala, a perfect whole. "This is the church as it's meant to be," my spiritual mentor points out, "and that, over there, is the church that didn't adapt." The direction of his hand reveals the same circular objects, but none of them are connected, and a blustering, cold wind blows through their shattered windows and empty rooms littered with broken glass.

Toward the conclusion of my first year, I prepared to terminate my relationship with Fritz because the course with him was coming to an end. Shortly before our last meeting I had this dream: I am sitting across from Fritz in his office, and I begin to tell him that, although I learned a great deal from him for which I am grateful, it is time to say good-bye. Just as I utter these last words, the large, open window behind Fritz suddenly crashes to the floor, and with a loud noise shatters into a million pieces. Frankly, at the time, I did not understand the meaning of this dream, but when I related it to Fritz, he seemed most interested in what my unconscious was saying quite clearly—and loudly!— about the importance of our relationship and of his role as my spiritual guide. He humorously suggested that we not ignore the blatant message, but continue to meet on a less formal basis, and that he continue, as the dream revealed, to act as an open window on my soul.

Fritz was there for me in the following years until I completed my graduate studies and began a new life, now filled with the joys and conflicts of a two-career family and two young sons, John and Daniel, who have their own agendas and waking hours. But, despite my tiredness and the exhaustion that comes with a busy, conscious life, certain dreams and the mysterious figures within them continue to cry out, "Pay attention!"

The World of Dreams

Because of the creative insights of psychotherapists such as Jung and the publication of more articles in both scholarly journals and popular magazines on the topic of dreams, people today are becoming more interested in dreams and dream interpretation. Researchers tell us that dreaming is a very normal phenomenon; everyone dreams, possibly four or five times nightly, though most of us don't always remember our dreams unless they are exceptionally vivid, repetitive or in the frightening category of nightmares. Experiments in dream research have also shown that a dream-deprived person will become sick, physically and emotionally, in three to six days. Dreams evidently function internally as healing agents and resources of renewed energy whether we acknowledge them consciously or not. Those who have studied mythology, primitive cultures, Jungian psychology and especially our own Judeo-Christian history can tell us, however, that it is to our physical, psychological, emotional and spiritual advantage to take our dreams seriously and attempt to understand them.

Our contemporary society, of course, is neither the first to take the realm of dreams seriously, nor the first to attempt to understand its mysterious language. Primitive tribes, for example, often believed that the vocation of shaman or spiritual leader was initiated through a dream encounter with a mysterious being or the soul of an ancestor, and that guidance continued for the shaman through his or her dreams. Mircea Eliade's *Shamanism: Archaic Techniques of Ecstasy* tells us:

> It is in dreams that the pure sacred life is entered and direct relations with the gods, spirits, and ancestral souls are reestablished. It is always in dreams that historical time is abolished and the mythical time regained—which allows the future shaman to witness the beginnings of the world and hence to become contemporary not only with the cosmogony but also with the primordial mythical revelations.

As we know from the story of Patrick and his discovery of vocation through his dreams, the early Celtic Christians also had a deep respect for dreams, possibly derived from the pagan druids and

shamans who preceded them. The desert tradition of spiritual
mentoring has numerous stories of the *abbas* and *ammas* filled
with mention of dreams. Native American Indians have similar
traditions advising them especially to value those dreams that
come at the particular life stages of puberty, young adulthood,
mid-life and old age. Other early civilizations, such as the Greek
and Roman, held a deep respect for the mysterious contents of
dreams.

While we are becoming increasingly aware of some of this
psychological, sociological and historical research related to
dreams, many people are unaware that dreams have also been an
intimate part of the history of the People of God, a spiritual heritage encompassing the Old and New Testaments as well as the
Christian churches of both the West and East. Before examining
what Jung can teach us about dreams and what we can learn from
our dream figures as potential spiritual mentors, let us briefly explore some of that rich and diverse history of Judeo-Christian spirituality, beginning with the stories found in our scriptures. What
we will find there, as other studies of history and various cultures
have shown, is that respect for dreams and dream interpretation is
definitely not a fad just now becoming popular in Western culture.
We will also discover that the deepest and most healthy aspects of
Christian growth and spirituality are often given guidance through
our dreams.

Dreams and Our Spiritual Heritage

From the opening pages of the Old Testament through the
Acts of the Apostles the reality of dreams and dream-like visions is
found. Without regard to the age of the dreamer, it seems, prom-
ises are given and vocations are discerned through dreams. The
Book of Genesis recounts the dream of Abram, who at 75 is asked
by God to leave country, family and father's house "for a land I
will show you." In his dream Abram is reassured that although his
descendants will be exiles and slaves in a land not their own, they
will eventually experience liberation (Gn 15:12-16). Evidently the
gift of vivid dreams can live on through the generations as a family
inheritance, for we also find the grandson of Abraham and Sarah,

Jacob, receiving the powerful dream of a ladder, "standing on the ground with its top reaching to heaven; and there were angels going up it and coming down." Yahweh was standing over him, we are told, and repeats in the dream the promise of his fidelity which he had originally made to Jacob's grandparents (Gn 28:10-22). Joseph, the son Jacob loved "more than all of his other sons," continues the family tradition of dreaming. He is sold into slavery by his jealous brothers, precisely because of his dream in which their sheaves of grain "bow to my sheaf" (Gn 37:5-11). Although Joseph evidently lacks sensitivity to his dream's contents—he naively (or egotistically) shares it with them—his story happily ends with reconciliation with his brothers and the blessing of his father.

Joseph's story in the Book of Genesis and Daniel's in the book of that name confirm what happens to those who begin to listen to their dreams: They often become spiritual mentors helping others in their discernment. Joseph did so with Pharaoh and won his approval. Daniel, a man who has "the gift of interpreting every kind of vision and dream" (Dn 1:17-18), does the same for Nebuchadnezzar. Like his ancestors in faith, Daniel also dreams in powerful images, the most famous of his dreams later associated with the coming of the Messiah:

> I gazed into the visions of the night.
> And I saw, coming on the clouds of heaven,
> one like a son of man. . . .
> On him was conferred sovereignty,
> glory and kingship,
> and men of all peoples, nations and languages became his
>   servants (Dn 7:13-15).

Other references to dreams as expressions of God's care and fidelity can be found throughout the Old Testament. In the Book of Judges (7:12-15) and the Book of Esther it is clear that people respected the importance of dreams, and appreciated, as the Book of Job tells us, that God "speaks by dreams, and visions that come in the night" (Jb 33:14-17). Perhaps one of the most beautiful of dream stories is that of Solomon, when Yahweh invites him to ask whatever he desires. Solomon gratefully and humbly replies:

You showed great kindness to your servant, David, my father, when he lived his life before you in faithfulness and
justice and integrity of heart. . . . But I am a very young
man, unskilled in leadership. . . . Give your servant a heart
to understand how to discern between good and evil, for
who could govern this people of yours that is so great?

The scriptures tell us that Yahweh was pleased with Solomon's simple, yet profound request for a discerning heart, and in
turn told Solomon, "I give you a heart wise and shrewd as none
before you has had and none will have after you" (1 Kgs 3:4-12).
Then, Solomon awoke. "It was a dream," we are told, and yet,
perhaps precisely because of his ancestors' experiences, he knew
that it was not "just a dream," but a promise of God's personal
fidelity and, thus, a message of hope.

The books of the New Testament contain numerous references
to dreams or dream-like visions, especially related to significant
events in the life of Jesus and the early church. In the gospel of
Matthew especially we find dreams associated with Jesus' birth,
the inauguration of his public ministry and his passion. Almost
from the start of that gospel, poor, bewildered Joseph receives
guidance from an unexpected and quite assertive angel, who acts
as a spiritual mentor in a series of dreams—telling him to take
Mary as his wife, despite her pregnancy, to name the child Jesus,
to take both into Egypt after the child's birth, and then finally to
return to Nazareth when Herod has died. Joseph, perhaps remembering the dream legacy of his ancestors, consistently does "what
the angel of the Lord had told him to do" (Mt 1:18-24), as do the
Magi when they are warned in a dream not to go back to Herod and
reveal where the child Jesus lives. Both Joseph's and the Magi's
trust in and response to dreams contain two lessons for us: We
need to respond through action to our own dream images, and
dream figures often offer guidance to those who listen to them,
especially during times of crisis or transition when a child of
ours—possibly a new project, a creative venture, a different direction in our life—is waiting to be born or to be protected from harm.

Although there is no apparent record of dreams as such in the
adult life of Jesus, the synoptic gospels do equate some of the more

significant events in Jesus' ministry, passion and resurrection with dream-like visions, not unlike those visions and dreams primitive shamans experience at certain stages before becoming healers and guides of their tribes. We can discern this at Jesus' baptism, "Suddenly the heavens opened and he saw the Spirit of God descending like a dove and coming down on him." A voice spoke from the heavens, "This is my Son, the Beloved; my favor rests on him" (cf. Mt 3:16-17, Mk 1:9 and Lk 3:21); in the wilderness when he is tempted by the devil (Mt 4:1-11); in the story of the transfiguration when Peter, John and James, "heavy with sleep," see Moses and Elijah "appearing in glory" and "speaking of his passing," converse with their friend (Lk 9:28-36). In some ways this latter sequence, as well as the dream of Pontius Pilate's wife, warning that her husband have "nothing to do with that man" (Mt 27:19), give us intimations of how dreams at times seem to transcend our human parameters of time and space, forewarning us of the future.

In the accounts after Jesus' resurrection and ascension, and the burst of new life at Pentecost, we find the apostles, perhaps too tired from their travels and too worn out from their ministries, not acknowledging or remembering their dreams. Both Paul and Peter, however, had very vivid experiences, again seemingly related to dream-like states, which offered them guidance regarding their discernment of vocation and their emerging ideas of church. Saul meets Jesus on the road to Damascus (Acts 9:1-9), and Peter has a vision on a rooftop in Jaffa that teaches him that the church needs to be more inclusive in its membership and ministries (Acts 10). Both experiences are dramatic conversion events for the two involved, especially considering their previous stubbornness and self-righteousness. All of us, of course, are the beneficiaries of their attentive listening and creative response to those visions, which they equated with the voice and presence of God.

When we consider what followed the unforgettable days of that early church, we will see how much the threads of later wisdom figures' dreams add light and depth to the ongoing beauty and color of the tapestry of our spiritual heritage. The patterns or themes that emerge from it can give us insights into the importance and interpretation of dreams.

One of the first patterns, already perceived in the scriptures, is the respect the People of God had for their dreams as sources of God's guidance and call. This respect is evident in the writings of the early Church Fathers who, like many of their pagan contemporaries in the Greco-Roman culture which they shared, maintained a healthy reverence for dreams. Tertullian, in a treatise on the soul, acknowledges that "almost the greater part of mankind derive their knowledge of God from dreams." Augustine's *Confessions* has numerous references to dreams, and Origen equated dreams with the activity of the divine Logos. Cyprian looked to his dreams for practical guidance in making decisions, while Athanasius, champion of orthodoxy against the Arians, states in *Against the Heathen* that in dreams the soul transcends the body and communicates directly with the angels of God.

Still, there is a distinct recognition throughout the history of Christian spirituality that although dreams can be equated with the presence and care of a loving God, there must be some discernment of their contents. This discernment process emerges as a definite theme in the early stages of the desert tradition of spiritual mentoring. Here in the stories and sayings of the *abbas* and *ammas* seeking God and self-knowledge in the wilderness, we find an emphasis on the importance of being able to tell the difference between good and bad spirits, some of which, they believed, appeared in dreams. There is, for example, the story of the hermit Abraham in *The Life of St. Mary the Harlot*; a huge and monstrous dragon appeared in his dreams. Because Abraham fails to discern that this dragon is a symbol of the power of evil, which is beginning to take over the life of his niece Mary, she becomes a whore and is only rescued by him some years later when he recognizes his mistake.

Another desert father, Diodochus of Photike, believed that dreams because of God's love "are unerring criteria" of the soul's health; yet one must at the same time attempt to discern whether specific dreams are from God or from the devil. How can we tell the difference? According to Diodochus, "good dreams" are those associated with joy and gentleness, while "demonic fantasies" bring about discontinuity and turmoil. Even here, however, he admits that it is not always easy to make those distinctions, since sometimes even good dreams "do not bring joy to the soul, but produce in it a sweet sadness and tears." He adds, "But this happens only to those who are far advanced in humility." Faced with the uncertainty of how to interpret our dreams, what are we to do? St. Basil evidently prayed that his sleep not be troubled by dreams! The desert wisdom figures advocate prayer for God's assistance in making any discernment, as well as the help of a spiritual mentor to make that discernment more reliable.

Another pattern in the history of Christian spirituality is the frequency with which dreams are associated with the discovery of a person's vocation. This is especially clear when we consider the life stories of those who founded monastic or religious communities. Dreams, as we've seen, had a profound effect on Patrick, the founder of Irish monasticism. There was also Pachomius, a pioneer in the establishment of monasteries in Egypt, who received a dream that changed his life in A.D. 313 when he was baptized:

> The night he was made worthy of the mystery (of Christ), he had a dream. He saw the dew of heaven descend upon him. When the dew had collected in his right hand and turned into solid honey and the honey had dropped onto the ground, he heard someone say to him, "Understand what is happening, for it will happen to you later." Then moved by the love of God, he sought to become a monk.

Interpreting the dream as a sign from God of his being called to be food and nourishment for others, Pachomius began his ascetic life by becoming an apprentice to the *abba* Palamon and learning from him to serve the poor. This same Pachomius went on to teach others about the ideal of holiness as compassion and purity of heart. Because of him and others like him, there came to be, as Athanasius's *Life of Antony* tells us, "monasteries in the mountains and the desert was made a city by monks."

The legends surrounding the layman Francis, who founded the Franciscan Order, also refer to the importance of dreams in the discernment of vocation. Anyone who has visited Assisi and seen the portrayal of Francis' dreams in the colorful frescoes of the artist Giotto in the Basilica's Upper Church is aware how much influence dreams had on Francis' life, conversion and ministry. In addition, the frescoes show that even popes were influenced by dreams. In Giotto's art Pope Innocent III dreams that the Lateran Basilica is about to collapse until a little poor man, Francis, puts his shoulders to the building and prevents it from falling. Gregory IX, in doubt about the stigmata of Francis, also dreams that Francis appears to him and fills an empty vial with blood that comes from the wound in his side, thus confirming his stigmata's authenticity. One series of dreams, which Francis himself had, came to him as a young soldier, before his conversion, and included a voice addressing him, "Turn around!" After his conversion, whether in a dream or vision, he was given further guidance in the church of San Damian when the image of the crucifix told him, "Francis, don't you see my house is in ruins? Go and restore it." Trembling with excitement, Francis replied, "Gladly, will I do so, dear Lord!" If we have attempted to interpret the meaning of our dreams, we know how difficult that can be at times, and what is especially heartening about this last dream or vision is that Francis misinterpreted it. According to historians he initially thought that he was to rebuild the church of San Damian itself, rather than interpreting Jesus' command to restore the institutional church by bringing new life and a new form of spirituality into it. Francis spent some time in the task of the San Damian restoration before realizing that his discernment process of the dream or vision needed revising.

Another pattern emerges in Christian history regarding dreams. They are sometimes associated with the future, as if they somehow stand outside of time, capable of giving us insight into future happenings. Augustine describes in his *Confessions* how his mother, Monica, so concerned about him before his conversion, was reassured in a dream that he would become a Christian. In Book III, chapter 11, we are told:

> In her dream she was standing on a sort of wooden ruler, and there came to her a very beautiful young man with a happy face, smiling at her, though she herself was sad and

> overcome with her sorrow. He then asked her [his purpose
> being, as is usual in these visions, to instruct her rather than
> to be instructed] why it was that she was so sad, and she
> replied that she was weeping for my perdition. Then he told
> her to have no fear and instructed her to look carefully and
> see "that where she was, I was too," and when she did look
> she saw me standing close by her on the same ruler.

When Monica related the dream to Augustine, he initially denied
that it had any meaning. Only later, after his conversion, did he
admit the wisdom of the dream. What is also of interest in his description is his own acknowledgement that dream figures have a
purpose when they appear in our dreams: to instruct the dreamer,
or in this case, to reassure an anxious mother that the future was
guided by God's providence.

Premonitions of death can also be perceived in certain famous
dreams. In the history of the United States various biographies of
Lincoln tell of his dreams the last weeks of his life, warning him of
his future assassination. Unfortunately he dismissed them as
"only dreams." A dream recorded by Thomas Merton in his journal also can be discerned, in retrospect, as the premonition of an
early death. In *Conjectures of a Guilty Bystander*, published in
1965, three years before his sudden death in Thailand, he describes a dream:

> I dreamt I was lost in a great city and was walking "toward
> the center" without quite knowing where I was going. Sud-
> denly I came to a dead end, but on a height, looking out a
> great bay, an arm of the harbor, I saw a whole section of the
> city spread out before me.

A paragraph later he adds: "I think sometimes that I may soon die,
though I am not yet old [47]." The juxtaposition of those words in
such close proximity becomes especially intriguing when we learn
what happened after Merton's death. His friend John Howard
Griffin received the camera and last roll of film Merton had taken
with him on his trip to the East, and developed the pictures with
great care. In *A Hidden Wholeness: The Visual World of Thomas*

Merton, Griffin tells us that when he held up one of the last photographs taken by Merton:

> I looked through Merton's eyes on a scene viewed from a high place, downward past the edge of a building and a foreground of shore across a broad body of water from which reflected sunlight glinted back into the viewer's eyes—a universal, all-embracing view of men and boats and water, seen from the perspective of height and distance....His photograph of the Bangkok River, the one that was in his camera at the time of his death and the one I had enlarged was an exact depiction of that dream.

Griffin was astounded by the synchronicity of the earlier journal entry and the picture.

Although dreams sometimes point to our mortality or that of our loved ones, they also paradoxically seem to affirm at times that there is more to life than death; that God is with us especially when we face that ultimate life transition; and that in some mysterious way we shall survive. In her famous autobiography, *The Story of a Soul*, Therese of Lisieux describes a dream that came to her shortly before she died, even though she acknowledges that she thought "dreams weren't for unimportant souls like mine." This dream, which foretold that she did not have long to live, also reassured her that God was very pleased with her life:

> At dawn next morning, May 10, I dreamt I was in the corridor, walking alone with Reverend Mother. Suddenly, without knowing how they had got there, I saw three Carmelite nuns, wearing their mantles and long veils. I knew they were from heaven. . . . instantly, I recognized the Venerable Mother Anne of Jesus, the foundress of Carmel in France. . . . She caressed me and, moved by her love, I ventured to say: "I implore you, Mother, to tell me if God is going to leave me on earth for long. Will He come for me soon?" She gave me a tender smile: "Yes, soon . . . soon. I promise you." I went on: "Tell me also, Mother, if God is pleased with me. Does He want anything from me beyond my poor little deeds and longings?" As I spoke, her face

shone with a new splendour and her gaze grew even more tender. She said: "God asks nothing more from you. He is pleased, very pleased." She took my head between her hands and I cannot give you any idea of the sweetness of her love for me. I was aflame with joy, but . . . I woke up. This dream made me indescribably happy, and although several months have passed, its freshness and heavenly charm are still sharp in my memory.

In the beautiful book of Russian spirituality, *The Way of the Pilgrim*, we also find a story about dreams and the immortality of those we love. In this story another layman, an anonymous Russian pilgrim, goes in search of someone who can teach him how to pray. He finally finds a *starets*, a spiritual guide, who acquaints him with the practice of *hesychasm*, the continuous prayer of the heart. Then his friend dies unexpectedly, leaving him discouraged and feeling abandoned. The pilgrim, however, soon discovers with wonder and gratitude that his spiritual mentor lives on in his dreams, guiding him there as much as he had when he was physically alive:

> And then I dreamed that I was in my departed *starets'* cell, and that he was explaining the *Philokalia* to me. "The holy book is full of profound wisdom," he was saying. "It is a secret treasury of the meaning of the hidden judgments of God. . . . It gives to each such guidance as he needs. . . . In [the writings of] these Fathers there are full directions and teaching on interior prayer of the heart, in a form which everyone can understand."

It was one dream among others that eventually helped transform the pilgrim from a man in search of a spiritual mentor to a mentor himself.

In addition to dreams that deal with future happenings and those that point to a reality greater than death, yet another pattern that emerges is the manner in which dreams provide resources for creativity. John Bunyan's memorable characters in *The Pilgrim's Progress*, for example, evidently came to the Puritan author as a result of dreams while imprisoned for his beliefs. The opening lines of his spiritual classic begin with this scene:

> As I walked through the wilderness of this world, I lighted
> on a certain place, where was a den; and I laid me down in
> that place to sleep: and as I slept I dreamed a dream. I
> dreamed, and behold I saw a man clothed with rags, stand-
> ing in a certain place, with his face from his own house, a
> book in his hand, and a great burden upon his back.

Thus we are introduced to the journey of Christian, who, representing all Christians, seeks through terrors and trials to reach
the Celestial City. His guides include Greatheart, Discretion, Pi-
ety and especially Charity and Hopeful. Christian reaches his des-
tination, and Bunyan's characters live on for us precisely because
Bunyan took time to carry on a dialogue in his imagination with the
figures of his dreams.

C. S. Lewis evidently did the same. According to his biographer and friend, Roger Lancelyn Green, many ideas for scenes
and characters in Lewis' stories originated in the Oxford professor's dreams and nightmares. Green writes in James Como's
book, *C. S. Lewis at the Breakfast Table*,

> When we were discussing dreams and the imaginative liter-
> ary use to be made of them, I complained that though I
> dreamed frequently, I seldom remembered anything from
> my dreams. I shall never forget the vehemence with which
> he turned on me and exclaimed: "Then you may thank God
> that you don't!" And he went on to explain that he had suf-
> fered most of his life from appalling nightmares—which he
> remembered only too well when he awakened.

As a result of such dream episodes Lewis wrote convincingly about
"The Dark Island" in *The Voyage of the Dawn Treader* and of
"The Head" in *That Hideous Strength*. Among some of the other
dream images that appeared in his works, according to Green, were
the Brown Girls of *The Pilgrim's Regress*, and Aslan, the beloved
lion and Christ-figure of the Narnian Tales. He even subtitled a
novel, *The Great Divorce*, "A Dream." It is unfortunate for Lewis
that he had such horrifying nightmares, but in a very real way we
are beneficiaries of those frightening dream episodes.

Though other patterns related to dreams appear in our Judeo-

Christian history, we can see that dreams have been consistently affirmed, albeit with certain reservations, as having religious significance. Ours is not the first age to take our dreams seriously and attempt to decipher their meaning. All sorts of God's pilgrim people paid attention to them—our ancestors in faith of both Testaments, Old and New, the early Church Fathers and desert wisdom figures, Irish saints and founders of religious communities, medieval mystics and anchoresses, Puritan and Russian pilgrims, modern monks and spiritual guides. Still, it has only been recently, primarily due to the insights of Freud and especially Jung, that many Christians have begun to listen to their dreams and reclaim their spiritual heritage.

Jung's Significant Contribution

In *The Chosen* Chaim Potok tells us that "what's inside us is the biggest mystery of all." If Julian of Norwich in 14th-century England could describe in her writings how God had opened her spiritual eyes in a series of visions or "revelations" and revealed "my soul in the midst of my heart"—a soul "as wide as if it were a kingdom" or "a fine city"; if Teresa of Avila in 16th-century Spain could compare the soul to "a castle made entirely out of a diamond or of very clear crystal, in which there are many rooms," it was Carl Jung in Zurich, Switzerland, who revealed to the 20th century the mysterious depth and vast, uncharted dimensions of the soul.

Defining the soul or *psyche*, the Greek word for "soul," as all those conscious and unconscious processes that make us who we are, Jung believed that the soul is androgynous, containing both masculine and feminine elements that each sex must integrate in order to become a more balanced person. He also posited that the human soul is born with a past: "Our souls as well as our bodies are composed of individual elements which were all already present in the ranks of our ancestors. The 'newness' in the individual psyche is an endlessly varied recombination of age-old components." And he adds a statement of great importance for anyone interested in Jungian psychology, the history of spirituality and spiritual mentoring: "We are very far from having finished completely with the Middle Ages, classical antiquity, and primitivity, as our modern psyches pretend." Jung said that many moderns were physically and emotionally ill because of what he called "loss of soul," being out of touch with the unconscious side of ourselves, our roots, our past, our traditions. Jung's task, as he saw it, was to help people re-connect not only with their pasts, but to begin the process of integrating the conscious and unconscious parts of themselves. While our consciousness is dominated by the ego, the center of consciousness, our unconscious contains personal and collective archetypal psychic contents, which in our dreams take on definite personalities. The process by which a person becomes an autonomous and psychological individual, more inner-directed than outer-controlled, Jung called individuation. This inherently spiritual process by which a personality is formed is not narcissism or mere self-indulgence, but its opposite. Agreeing with the author of Ecclesiasticus that "gold is tested in the fire, and chosen men [and women] in the furnace of humiliation" (Sir 2:1-5), Jung stated that individuation necessarily involves the willingness "to be near the fire," to undergo the suffering of a diminution of the ego and the emergence of the greater Self or personality waiting to be born. What is interesting, from the perspective of a Christian theologian, is that Jung, as psychiatrist, speaks of Christ as the archetype of this greater Self, a symbol of the wholeness and integration all people need to seek, especially in their second half of life. As Jung assumed, and Jesus' own life reveals, this process involves the courage to face the unknown, the darkness within. It also presupposes a commitment to discovering the truths about oneself, which at times can be very painful and disconcerting. The goal of the individuation process as described by Jung is to achieve a kind of mid-point of the personality, where "the center of the total personality no longer coincides with the ego, but with a point midway between the conscious and the unconscious." Jung gave this center the name Self.

A dream, according to Jung, is "a little hidden door in the innermost and most secret recesses of the soul," and when we begin to pay attention to the figures, plots and stories that appear in our dreams, we gain entrance into that mysterious reality we call soul. Jung said that there were two categories of dreams to watch for: 1) little dreams, those ordinary types that provide insight into our daily conflicts, anxieties and creative potentials; and, 2) big dreams, the vivid, sometimes repetitive dreams that often come at specific turning points in our lives. The latter, as we have already documented in the lives of the wisdom figures from our Judeo-Christian heritage, can give us insight into our vocation and the larger dream dimensions of our emerging Self. Jung was convinced that "natural transformation processes announce themselves mainly in dreams," and thus anyone doing spiritual mentoring should be particularly attentive to the presence and possible meanings of big dreams because of the directions they might give in discerning future paths.

Whether little or big, each type of dream contains a great variety of figures, personalities and archetypal images. These inner constellations of psychic energies and memories, containing a great deal of psychic power, have the potential for bringing about ongoing transformation—or its opposite. When recognized, befriended and integrated into our consciousness, they can bring about a personality change, sometimes quite significant; if left unrecognized or repressed, we can experience a great deal of discomfort or outright destruction in our lives. Jung gives some of these dream figures specific names. *Animus* is the masculine side of a woman's personality in need of integration; *anima* is the feminine side of males. The *shadow* refers to all those unknown parts of ourselves that we have rejected and repressed out of fear, hatred or painful memories, and which we often project on others rather than seek to integrate within ourselves. This shadow side, paradoxically, also contains our creative potential, and as fairy tales such an "The Ugly Duckling" or "Cinderella" often show, it is when the shadow is accepted and loved, kissed as it were, that transformation into something very positive occurs. Another figure is the Self, already referred to, whom Jung describes as "the inner friend of the soul." Frequently in contrast to the Self in our dreams is the *persona*, the side of our personality (actually part of our ego) that masks from others—and ourselves—who we really are, especially when we identify too closely with a role or job description rather than the Self we are meant to be.

All of these figures take on the faces and characters of different people who in our dreams may be quite familiar or very strange and unknown. Jung advises males to pay special attention to the women in their dreams, for they may be portraying aspects of the feminine side in need of integration; females need to watch for the male figures, who may or may not be known. The shadow is another archetype that needs our special care because of its potential for transformation, self-acceptance and inner healing. He or she may appear as a despicable, poor, crippled or disfigured person, a wounded animal, a member of another race, an unknown assailant with a gun, a witch, a murderer. The clue often to our shadow is the repugnance or fear we show it in the dream. According to Jung, the shadow figure is always of the same sex as the dreamer.

The Self may appear as someone we respect, a healer, teacher, mentor, guide, a wise old woman or man, a person with seemingly mythic proportions. Jung and others clearly warn us not to *consciously* identify with this figure alone, for such archetypes are inherently one-sided and must always be balanced by another side. If we identify, for example, with a healer archetype in our work or ministry (a common identification for those who seek to be of help to others), this archetype needs to include a wounded side. Henri Nouwen's *The Wounded Healer* is based upon this insight. Not to recognize and accept our wounded, limited side in ministry will drive us mad, sometimes literally, or at least cause the sickness called burn-out.

As sources of transformation these archetypes appear in many guises and disguises. Sometimes these figures also have mythic proportions, revealing what Jung posited as "the Collective Unconscious," that phenomenon, transcending our individual psyches, containing the whole spiritual heritage of humankind's evolution, "born anew in the brain structure of every individual." It is the source of "the instinctual forces of the psyche and of the forms or categories that regulate them, namely the archetypes." Somehow this Collective Unconscious overlaps our personal unconscious and makes itself known in our dreams. An example of one such archetype might be an unfamiliar figure who appears unannounced and who seems to be from a different time or culture. Jung says that "the more vivid they are, the more they will be colored by particularly strong feeling-tones." They can impress, influence and fascinate us with their appearance, dress, the color of their hair or the depth of their personalities. Sometimes they appear to be our greater Self; often they seem to be associated with certain interior ages, stages or seasons of our lives, not always chronological, in need of integration. A baby or young child who appears in our dreams may be an intimation of the start of new life or a new stage in our development; he or she may be pointing to new sources of creativity that we have not yet recognized. A youth or Adonis-like figure may symbolize some naive vitality or inner strength waiting to be touched. A strong adult male figure, like the Greek god Zeus, may represent our need, whether we are male or female, to claim our competence and power or, depending upon the dream, may show how we have been abusing the power we already have. A voluptuous feminine figure, like the goddess Aphrodite, may speak to us, if we are male, of the transforming power of eros that awaits our passionate embrace, or if we are female, of a sexuality in need of development. A parent figure may be telling us of nurturing and protective abilities; a hero or heroine of a person's qualities we unconsciously seek to emulate; a shaman or priest of healing and religious powers perhaps untapped; a clown or fool figure of our need to balance an over-serious dedication or "workaholism" with play. An old man or woman, representing a wisdom figure, may be implicitly calling us to recognize our interior sources of wisdom.

However archetypes appear in our dreams, they are all aspects of our inner self and all potential inner friends of the soul. To recognize their faces as those of our parents, spouses, colleagues, friends and enemies is not necessarily to gain insight into *those* people's lives and personalities, although that may occasionally occur; rather, they invite us to examine the parts of *our* interior life that they are revealing, which when brought into greater consciousness, can make us more whole. My inner wounded child, for example, first appeared in the guise of my son John. In a series

of dreams, repetitive in their horror, I dreamt that I had lost him
and was desperately searching for him. It was only when I discussed with my spiritual guide what aspect of my younger life John
represented that the horrible dreams eventually disappeared. Once
I had named my own wounded interior child, healing could begin,
and "John" was no longer "lost." Other people whom I easily
recognized in my dreams represented some part of me: my
mother, the nurturing and sometimes overly co-dependent side;
my wife, the feminine wisdom side seemingly often in conflict
with the masculine; the crippled, disfigured person, so apparently
unacceptable, who is my shadow.

All our dream figures, the archetypes with faces we recognize
immediately or those for whom we have no notion of identity, can
be mentors to us, teaching us about the unknown parts of who we
are, guiding us to new perspectives of self and perceptions of vocation. Whether recognized or not, as strangers they often come,
like the Old and New Testament stories of unknown visitors and
assertive angels, from God. Their purpose is to teach us something
about ourself that we do not now consciously know, to heal those
parts of us in need of reconciliation, or to confirm what it is we are
perhaps just beginning to understand. They seek to integrate our
dark sides with the light and make us aware of our power to com-
mit evil, self-destructive deeds, as well as to respond courageously to our call to holiness. They can be guides to new harmony
and a New Jerusalem, and as with St. Peter's experience with
God, they do not always lead us to a place where we would like to
go.

A Process of Discerning the Meaning of Dream Images

We need not know all the terminology proposed by Jung, or be
psychologists ourselves, to have our dream figures act as spiritual
mentors to us. Although some acquaintance with theories of Jungian psychology and dream interpretation can help, what we need
most is the desire to remember our dreams and the courage to be-
friend the figures in them—rather than keeping them at arms
length or quickly forgetting that they exist at all. "Oh, that was
only a dream" is a not-so-subtle form of denial that probably

harms the dreamer more than those who populate our dreams. Granted, we may at first be somewhat apprehensive of what they might reveal about us, or we may keep putting off making a commitment to learn from them. But, unless we act on that desire to know and make that commitment to personal growth, none of the following will work. In many ways naming our dream figures, as Adam and Eve named the animals in the Garden, establishes a relationship with them, a form of dialogue in which their power over us no longer leads to self-destructive feelings or behavior against others on whom we have projected our own problems or prejudices.

Another important dynamic of befriending our dreams as sources of psychological and spiritual wisdom is to be patient with them and with ourselves from the start. Like learning a foreign language, familiarity with the words, phrases, symbols and content only comes with time and practice. Even then we cannot expect, as when we visit a foreign land, to be totally at ease with everything we meet.

With these precautions in mind, let me propose a process in which dream figures may become important spiritual mentors. This discernment process can ultimately lead to greater self-awareness, the foundation of an authentic spirituality of care. This process contains the following stages: 1) recording the dream; 2) naming the inner guides; 3) conversing with and listening to them; and 4) responding through specific actions or activities.

Presupposing that we have decided to take the risk involved with greater self-knowledge and have made the commitment to enter into our own individuation process, let us begin.

1) *Recording the Dream:* This stage contains a number of steps. The first step is to place a pen and paper next to the bed or in close proximity to it. Some people prefer a tape recorder to writing, and that too, if it is easily accessible, can be a way of recording our dreams immediately upon waking. Unrecorded dreams, unless unusually vivid, disappear from our consciousness in a very short time, so it is necessary to have something to write on or speak into for later reflection and dialogue.

Second, before going to sleep we consciously ask God to help us remember our dreams so that they can act as guides to our souls. In some mysterious way this *conscious* request for help is often granted; the request itself seems to trigger in us the ability to remember those dreams we really need to recall.

Third, upon awakening, *yet without being fully awake*, we need to record what we remember of the preceding night's dreams. Since our dreams seem to coincide with the structure of a good play or story, this recording can be aided by asking ourselves the following questions associated with the various stages of dreams which Jung has named:

a. *the exposition:* Where and with whom does the dream begin? What figures appear in it initially? Who is there and where do we find ourselves? In what sort of land or place does the action start? Are they familiar places or people? Do we recognize anything significant or distinct about them?

b. *plot development:* What tension or conflict arises in the dream as it unfolds? Are there specific actions that increase the drama? Do words spoken by the figures bring about some response? Is there tension or conflict evident, or is it a scene of tranquility and peace? What is going on as the plot unravels?

c. *culmination:* What actions taken in the dream constitute a turning point? Does something decisive happen in the dream? Who or what is involved? Is there anything or anyone who stands out, who is significant in some way?

d. *lysis:* What is the dream's conclusion? How and with whom does it end? Where does it leave us? With what feelings do we awake? Fear, serenity, anger, joy, guilt, relief? Now that we have recorded as much of the dream with its plot and figures as we can remember, we can go on to the next stage.

2) *Naming the Inner Guides:* This stage involves two movements: making associations, and giving the dream figures names. First, we need to ask the questions related to the specific contents of the dream and allow our past and present experiences to come to mind.

Where the action of the dream occurred: Can I name the

country or place? What associations can I make with this place? Have I ever lived there; if so, how old was I and what was going on then? What feelings do I have toward this time in my life? If it is not familiar to me, what country or place would I associate it with? what century or time? what culture or historical period? What comes to mind when I reflect upon it?

The figures in my dream: If they are familiar to me, who are they and what relationship do I have with them in my conscious life? Do they remind me of certain people from my past or present life? In what ways are they possibly significant? What aspect of myself could they represent? What are my feelings, both positive and negative, toward them?

If they are not familiar, what persons, countries or historical periods do they remind me of? Are their clothes of a special design or color? If so, what do I think of when I reflect on the design; what significance does the color have for me?

In making our associations we need to give ourselves time to recall our past and present life. In addition to our own experiences and memories, as important as they are, some knowledge of scripture and our spiritual heritage can help, as can knowledge of psychology, the classics, mythology and the meaning of symbols. This can be an ongoing form of education that adds to effective dream interpretation as we grow older. All can contribute to our eventually naming the places and especially the figures about which we have dreamed.

After questioning who has appeared and what has happened in our dreams, and what associations we can make with their contents, we need to actually give names to the figures that are especially memorable; some may keep reappearing in our dreams. This naming in a very real way is establishing a relationship of friendship with the figures, and thus inviting them to teach us something about ourselves. As in our conscious lives, strangers most often have little lasting effect on our lives. Naming them for ourselves, or confirming the name they already have in our conscious lives, reveals our willingness to be affected by them. Sometimes a name comes readily to mind; other times we need to wait and perhaps let the figure eventually reveal his or her name to us.

3) *Conversing With and Listening to Our Dream Figures:*   This stage is of crucial importance in our relationship with the images of our dreams. As with any friendship, if we are to experience a growth in intimacy and understanding, we need to cultivate a relationship of depth with the figures that have now been named. This means spending time with them, quiet time listening to what they have to tell us as spiritual mentors and friends. We must avoid a "how to interpret our dreams in one minute or less" mentality. Only in our patient waiting for dream figures to speak will they do so. We also must be willing to discuss with them the most personal aspects of our lives. However we approach this dialogue with them, we will need to draw upon our own patience, creative imagination and listening abilities. Because this conversation with them is so closely related to prayer, we will also need to turn to God, since ultimately all the guidance and the insights we gain from the dream images, of course, come from God.

We first need to find a quiet space in our day after the preceding night's dream(s) and set aside an adequate amount of time in which to dialogue. Journaling can be an important help in this listening and responding process. Once we have settled down, possibly opening with a prayer to clear our minds and hearts, we can begin to carry on a conversation in our imagination or through our writing. Address the dream mentor by name when beginning this stage. If we are just initiating a relationship with the dream mentor, we need to greet him or her with warmth, as we would any new acquaintance, and spend a little time being hospitable. Then we ask the mentor why he or she has entered our dreams, and what we can learn from our conscious dialogue. We need to let our imaginations flow in this dialogue; as St. Ignatius of Loyola believed, such creative listening can help us discover God. Feeling more at ease with the dream image, we allow whatever comes to mind. This encouragement of the creative imagination is very much related to the way we pray: We simply put ourselves consciously in the presence of God, and then in our letting go, allow the silence to speak. So, also with the dream mentor.

Let the mentor teach, counsel, heal and guide us in ways beyond the conscious or rational. Much of this unfolding conversation will depend upon our listening with the heart, the innermost center of our being, the place where we struggle to discern what it is we are called to do or be.

Sometimes this process is more than listening. It may mean a great deal of struggling with the image, as Jacob did with the angel. Sometimes this struggle may continue over an extended period of time rather than in only one quiet session. When we struggle to comprehend and accept, we need to be willing to wrestle, to get our clothes dirty and dishevelled, to lose our balance and right ourselves again. Sometimes we may just need to lie in the mud and slime for a while. At other times we may call directly on God's help, as did Daniel in the lions' den. Often it may mean just quietly turning to the dream mentor and listening courageously to what he or she may have to say.

Wherever the dream figure leads us, this stage comes to a conclusion when something that is said or received from the mentor finally "clicks"—makes sense at the visceral level, in our stomach, guts and heart. Only we can tell the meaning any one dream has or what any one dream mentor is trying to say—no one else can do that.

Although the conversation in our prayers and imagination can continue with certain significant dream figures who have appeared, the next step is doing what Joseph did with the angel who appeared in his dreams: "He did what the angel told him to do." That is, the next step is acting upon the guidance we have received.

4) *Our Responding Through Action:* The preceding stage usually ends with the question: What is it that I am asked to do as a result of this dream and the dialogue I have had with the dream mentor? At this stage of discerning our response, we are like both Martha and Mary in the gospel story—in need of our abilities to listen and to act with love. In seeking ways to respond to the insights we have gained we need to avoid grandiosity or unreal expectations. We need to ask: What one thing can I do today in response to the dream; what one activity can I change regarding my relationship with spouse, children, colleagues, friends? Sometimes ritualizing our insights and our desire for change can help us

respond to the dream. This ritual activity can take the form of drawing, painting, sculpting or writing a poem based on the dream images. It might consist of creating or purchasing an object to remind us of the new insight or new pattern of behavior to which we are committed. Or perhaps we might plan and participate in a celebration with appropriate symbols to honor the dream and its message. Another choice is simply writing a note to oneself about the dream's message and posting it in an obvious place as a reminder. If our dream or dreams come at a particular transition point in our lives, our response may have to be more dramatic and courageous, and involve a more extended period of time in which to make the changes to which our insights have led. In most cases, however, our dream mentors are not expecting us to perform unusually heroic acts. Discerning what response is most appropriate, of course, is not only up to us; we have included God as a third person in our dialogue. With God's help, then, we request the grace, power, ability to act. Above all, we need to pray, like Solomon, for the wisdom and the gift of a discerning heart.

Dreams as Windows on the Soul

Dreams are windows on the soul, reflecting ''through a mirror darkly'' the presence of a loving, caring God and the larger Self we are called to be. They reveal, as the English mystic Julian of Norwich discovered in her own revelations, ''that our life is all grounded and rooted in love,'' and that our God ''is our true spouse, and our soul his beloved wife.'' We often discern in the mysterious language of dreams God's loving presence as Mother and Father, Sister and Brother to us, and in so many unexpected ways they teach us, as true spiritual mentors, that ''all will be well, and all will be well, and all manner of things will be well.''

We need to pay attention to our dreams, not only those that come to us in the darkness of the night, but especially those that come at dawn. According to the poet Dante it is then that ''our minds, more pilgrim from the flesh, are less imprisoned by the bonds of thought and in their visions have prophetic power'' (*The Divine Comedy*). Whenever they occur, and evidently they may sometimes appear as visions in our waking hours as well, they have a reason for being there. They come, as did Dante's spiritual mentors, when we most need them, and then they disappear, as did Virgil and Beatrice, when they are no longer needed. They *seem to* vanish, that is; in reality they have become integrated into our inmost selves. We realize, as did Dante with his mentors, that in their helping us encounter "the love that moves the sun and the stars," they continue on, unobserved, as inner friends of the soul.

While welcoming our dream mentors with hospitality and remembering their presence with gratitude, we also approach them with a sense of proportion. Both our spiritual traditions and Jung himself teach us not to go too far overboard with our dreams. While they can be important resources for self-knowledge, creativity, ministry and ongoing conversion, and can provide a great deal of helpful mentoring especially at life transitions, we cannot ignore our conscious life or the communities of friends who dwell there. Dreams are one form of religious experience—but not the only one. To look for quick vocational answers from them, superficial ways of forecasting the future or egotistic ways of controlling God would be a form of superstition, which the church in its history has consistently warned people about. To do so would earn the justifiable scorn of a person like Gregory of Nyssa, who said "there are dreamers who consider the deceits of dreams more trustworthy than the teachings of the gospels, calling fantasies revelations."

Dreams can be from God, but they are not God. Neither are they some magical force, taking away our responsibility for engaging in a mature discernment process of their contents and of their meaning. In that process we need to turn for direction to other spiritual friends and mentors, to scripture, to disciplines such as Jungian or developmental psychology, and to our past wisdom figures as well. Any discernment of dreams cannot be done in isolation.

At the same time we also need to respect and reflect upon those people and events that live in our conscious lives and histories, to discuss what they too are telling us about God, ourselves, our vocation and the direction of our lives. Whether in dreams from the unconscious or events in our conscious lives, all of us are called to listen and to remember the places and people who have touched us by their love. As the Irish writer Sean O'Faolain has written: ''I think that if my life has had any shape it is this: I have gone on listening and remembering my youth, my country; to pallid clouds, caverns of green, rumbling river, whispering shell.''

To remember is an activity that not only expands our awareness of gifts received; it is a conscious activity in which we discover the living presence of the past and the mysterious reality of the soul. It unites the contemporary spiritual mentor with a spiritual community that transcends space and time.

SIX

A Link Between Ages

The authentic individual is neither an end nor a beginning but a link between ages, both memory and expectation. Only he [or she] who is an heir is qualified to be a pioneer.

Abraham Heschel, *Who Is Man?*

I remember a man who seemed the happiest when he held his children's children in his lap, talked with them, called their names and held them close. He blessed them; he made them feel precious and unique and chosen. Those moments for him were moments of great happiness—and yet, it seemed at times, moments of great sadness as well.

An old man, he would put them down from his lap and speak of the day when death would come and take him from their midst. He was not morbid about that fact, only sad that he would no longer be able to take them in his arms and bless them with his love. At other times, he would be playful, almost joking: "See that cemetery, there," he would point as we drove by. "How many people are dead and buried there do you think?" As a child, I

133

would try to guess: "Fifty? A hundred?" "No," he would smile, "all of them."

As a young man I would be asked the same question, but remembering, I already knew the answer. Then one time he added, "Someday I'll be buried there." Joking mixed with the reality of that future event. His life, in some ways, became an advent. It was not fear of death so much as sadness that he would have to leave us.

My grandfather John Lipetzky was born into a German family of seven children and raised near Springfield, Minnesota. He received his early education there and courted Mary Foy, whose Irish family numbered 16. They were married September 16, 1915, and in less than two weeks moved by train to the wide open spaces of North Dakota. Grandpa's brother Joe arrived on the next freight train after theirs, about half an hour later and helped them unload all of their possessions: five cows, four horses, a buggy, a stove and table, a wagon, and a fine new bedroom set. The following day the three of them hitched the horses to the wagon and drove out to the land that had been given to them as a wedding gift.

Grandma recalled to my mother many years later how lonely it was at first, how the house they moved into was full of bed-bugs, and how the only visitors were occasional Indians stopping by. My grandparents, however, were determined to stay. Within two years Grandpa's brothers Joe and Leo began farming nearby and not so much later the laughter and tears of small children interrupted the silence of the prairies and the stark loneliness. There were years of trying to make ends meet, watching crops eaten by grasshoppers and wiped out by drought, followed by years of celebrating their children's weddings and saying farewell to sons who were going off to war. One son, Cletus, never returned from that war; his body lies somewhere in the deep waters off the shores of Normandy. In the months following the notification that he was missing in action, Grandpa would sit quietly by the window, I am told, and wonder aloud: "I hope he didn't have to suffer. I wonder if he was killed immediately, or if he had to suffer." The presence of more and more grandchildren gradually seemed to ease his and Grandma's pain.

The two of them eventually retired from farming and moved to the nearby town of Kensal and into a house in which my parents now live, retired themselves. There, on visits with my children, I can still see the plot of land outside one of the windows that was Grandpa John's garden and sit at the table in the kitchen where Grandma Mary served me eggs and toast for breakfast.

Not long ago my family and I visited the graves of my grandparents in the cemetery that Grandpa used to point to as we drove by, located not many miles from the farm to which they had moved as pioneers. It was a Labor Day weekend, and the first time all of us were there together—my parents, Jo Anne, and our sons, John and Daniel. Gusts of wind were blowing the grass and clover and the branches of the trees that lined the cemetery. As the boys ran in and out of the blocks of marble and stone, then brought buckets of water from the hand-pumped well to water the flowers on the graves, I imagined that my grandfather would have appreciated their efforts. I could still picture him with his white hair standing in the fields of wheat that he'd planted, one hand over his eyes as he scanned the horizon at dusk, searching for signs of coming rain, the other hand grasping the wheat that he had just examined for signs of growth. I remembered my Grandma Mary too, out in the fields digging potatoes, with my cousin Barbara and myself, her two oldest grandchildren, trying to keep up. I remembered Grandma's recent death when John, then 5 years old, whispered to me in a tone of quiet wonderment while standing near her coffin, ''She's not breathing, Dad.''

How does a parent begin to explain that reality without conveying too much fear or too little respect for it? When is the right time to begin telling our children the stories of their ancestors? At what age will they appreciate these stories before indifference or the busyness of their own lives interfere?

As Jo Anne and I watched our children play, oblivious to the signs of death all around us, and listened to my mother identify the various people whose markers were visible and tell a story about each, I had for a brief moment a profound, intuitive, visceral experience of Grandpa's and Grandma's presence with us, a sense that here among us, living and dead, were ties that transcended space and time. My experience there that afternoon confirmed my belief, gift from my spiritual heritage, that in some mysterious way the past is a living thing, and we are bonded with other generations and other lives.

The Spiritual Community and Mentoring

This spiritual community, in which love overcomes physical limitations and makes us aware of a kinship with others that transcends death, is what this book has been about. We have discovered, or perhaps our original convictions have been confirmed, that relationships of ordinary mentoring and spiritual mentoring, which so often begin with grandparents and parents, teach us about ultimate realities. This spiritual communion of souls is another term for what the ancients called "the communion of saints"—not a community of perfect people, but a union of soul friends and sinners struggling to make sense of our lives and to live with some degree of integrity and hope. Like those who have gone before us, we search for identity and meaning after experiences of disorientation, disintegration and even despair. Like our ancestors, we seek ways of passing on a spiritual heritage to our children without forcing them to accept it as alien baggage on *their* sacred journeys through time. Like so many who have preceded us, we struggle to find wisdom, a wisdom not only of the mind, but of the heart, for we believe, as did they, that "in each generation she [wisdom] passes into holy souls, [and] makes them friends of God" (Wis 7:27).

Like our dream images at night or early dawn, certain friends do seem to come into our lives when we most need them. That, at least, is the experience of many who have taken time to reflect on their lives. Emilie Griffin refers to this synchronicity, the mystery of these unpredictable "coincidences," and how they are related to God's activity and grace. In *Clinging: The Experience of Prayer*, she writes:

> To "find" a spiritual friend is truly to be found, to be chased down, smoked out of one's hiding place in the corner of existence and brought into the center, swept into the blazing presence of God. . . . This love made into prayer and transformed by prayer is, I like to think, the friendship of the saints, in heaven and on earth.

C. S. Lewis reminds us of the same phenomenon:

> In friendship, we think we have chosen our peers. In reality, a few years' difference in the dates of our births, a few more miles between certain houses, the choice of one university instead of another . . . —any of these chances might have kept us apart. But for a Christian, there are, strictly speaking, no chances. A secret Master of the Ceremonies has been at work.

Whenever and however friendships are made or discovered, the spiritual community that comes into being as a result of them is in some mysterious way related to God's love for us and the mutual care we have for one another. Often it is only because of that human care and friendship that we have discovered the friendship of God.

Through the love of mentors we often discover the reality and the importance of the spiritual community itself. Whether we call them "ordinary" or "spiritual," mentors affirm at crucial times in our lives, through their acceptance of us, our own self-worth; they often help us find the capacity to survive our life transitions. Through their encouragement, questions and listening, we gain, as I did with Fritz, the ability to clarify and then pursue the dimensions of our dream. Sometimes when we feel especially lost, they help us to discern meaning, what theologian Paul Tillich equates with power and the Spirit of God; or, as Joe did for me, they help us to experience forgiveness, the greatest experience Tillich says anyone can have.

Most often mentors invite us to read our lives with as much care as those lives deserve. Through our reflection upon the good times and bad, the significant events and especially persons of our lives, we may even experience a change of heart. We may find a heart more compassionate and less judgmental, more humble and less self-righteous, more grateful and less resentful. Often, as a result of mentors helping us through stages of transformation, we encounter a deeper Self capable of mentoring others in return.

In many ways mentors may at first be people who seem to stand on a pedestal, those whom we admire from afar because they have the experience and wisdom we would like to possess, or because on an unconscious level they represent some aspect of our ideal self, which we carry within. Later, as we get to know them more intimately, we may come to identify with them precisely because of the depth of their human struggles to survive and, despite personal and/or professional conflicts or tragedies, to persist. It is at this stage that mutuality with mentors can begin to occur—when we have taken them down from the pedestal and allowed ourselves to encounter them as fellow travellers; that is, when we have begun to see them, as the Cambridge scientist saw Lewis, as a very good man to whom goodness did not come easily, or as many saw Robert Kennedy, as a passionate man who in the midst of his own grief wanted to make a difference in the life of the country. A sense of increasing mutuality in mentoring happens, however, not only when we begin to see our mentors as fully human, like ourselves, but when we as mentors begin to acknowledge how much our lives are changed by the talents and questions of those we mentor.

Mutuality in Mentoring

One of the greatest awarenesses that comes to those who mentor is the recognition of how much we receive from those who have sought us out. Because we have taken the time to be present with someone, we often discover that that person's search for answers is clarifying our own questions, and that we are not alone in our journey of faith and doubts. Frequently we find that the other's gifts of wisdom based upon life experiences, perhaps so different from our own, complement and support ours. We often come to see that the ones we are mentoring—no matter what their age—have become in some ways our teachers, mentors and guides.

The desert tradition, expressed in Norman Russell's *The Lives of the Desert Fathers*, has a story about a certain *abba* that confirms this dimension of mutuality. One of those early spiritual mentors, John of Lycopolis, tells of an ascetic who lived alone in the desert where he encountered many temptations. Eventually he returns to the life of community after a dream in which an angel advises him: ''God has accepted your repentance and has had mercy on you. In future take care that you are not deceived. The brethren to whom you gave spiritual counsel will come to console you, and they will bring you gifts. Welcome them, eat with them and always give thanks to God.''

For those of us who are spiritual mentors, the awareness that others bring us gifts and that we need to welcome them, eat with them and always give thanks to God is one of the most important aspects of our ministry. If we are to help people relate their everyday life of family, friendships, work and play to their spirituality; if we are to help guide them in their lives of prayer and compassionate solidarity with others; if we are to help them deepen the quality of their relationships with God and themselves, we need to invite them to do so by the example we give.

Christianity is not about denying our humanity, but, as the early Church Father Irenaeus said, about humanity "more fully alive." Christian spirituality is about being more whole and holy, and as other spiritual traditions affirm, about the discovery, acknowledgment and celebration of the sacred in our midst. It is a lifelong process of increased intimacy not only with God, but with all our brothers and sisters, especially those—the gospel of Jesus reminds us—who are poor, neglected, forgotten, abused.

Most especially, Christian spirituality acknowledges how much we have in common with one another. Whether we are female or male, married or single, lay or ordained, we all share an inner desire for establishing and maintaining human relationships and friendships. We all search for clarity about what we are to do with our lives. We all seek an integrity that transcends our failures and selfishness. We all desire a self-worth that is based upon some assurance that we are accepted in spite of our guilt and shame. We all experience, in our quietest moments and in the depth of our souls, the need for greater intimacy with God.

The spiritual mentor with such an inclusive vision invites this awareness of our mutual call to holiness and of our common destiny through his or her humanity. He or she invites this, not by being distant and aloof, but by being a friend who is willing to celebrate the good times as well as acknowledge the bad times in his or her life. While it is not necessarily advisable to share the whole of our lives with those we mentor, in general the more of ourselves we open to them, the more they will want and be able to share of themselves with us. The more honest, warm and genuine we are, the more we will elicit truthfulness and a relationship of greater depth, and thus, more fully receive what they have to offer.

If our attitude, perhaps not fully conscious, is that we are giving everything in our relationship and receiving nothing in return, resentments will develop that eventually alienate us from those we are mentoring. If our training or experience is perceived by us as somehow intrinsically greater and more worthwhile than another's, we will quickly adopt a condescending attitude in which there is little room for the development of reciprocity. When we do not acknowledge others' intelligence and maturity, we inevitably will treat them as inferiors or children who have nothing positive that they can contribute to make society, church or our own lives a better place. To welcome others and affirm their gifts is the opposite of paternalism, and when we are being effective spiritual mentors, those qualities of hospitality and affirmation lead inevitably to more gratitude in our lives and the lives of others—not less.

Mutuality in spiritual mentor and soul friend relationships brings out the best that is in each friend. Emotional and spiritual maturity is supported and develops more readily between those who see each other as having equal value. If C. S. Lewis, for example, had treated Bede Griffiths as "only a student" and never allowed Bede to get to know him outside of the classroom, neither man would have had the help of each other in discovering his own vocation and surrendering to a loving God. Recognizing that each had something to offer the other, that each had similar questions about God and the direction of their lives, both profited from the relationship; both grew in wisdom and holiness, and through their writings eventually helped many others discover the reality of God. When two people stop making comparisons about how much each other knows or doesn't know and simply acknowledge that they are engaged in a common search, mutuality emerges and both partners are transformed, sometimes dramatically.

Often, however, at least in the early stages of spiritual mentoring, the one who comes to the mentor for guidance or advice does not recognize the gifts and wisdom that he or she brings into the relationship. This is frequently something that the mentor intuitively has already discerned and can help the other discover. As a form of empowerment, this affirmation of gifts sometimes not yet named and certainly not claimed as one's own can be one of the greatest services we do for others. Another may be that of helping them name and claim the reality of the soul.

Dimensions of the Soul

Mentors and mentoring relationships are as diverse as the personalities involved, but for many mentors, especially spiritual mentors, one of the most essential tasks is to help others discover the dimensions of the soul, that all-encompassing reality greater than our conscious minds and more ancient than our egos. While our primary focus throughout this book has been on the ministry of mentoring, its underlying subject has been the reality of the soul. We have seen in our rich and varied traditions of spiritual mentoring, including our in-depth discussion of C. S. Lewis' life and ministry, how encounters with mentors can be equated with a communion of souls, that experience of intimacy and friendship transcending the state of enclosure and ignorance of which Haughton speaks. Other chapters on the Irish soul friend, our vocation as the call of life to the soul, and dream images as windows on the soul—all presupposed the existence of a reality greater than our conscious minds and yet intimately connected with our bodies.

Most contemporary Christian theologians do not write about that mysterious reality anymore, and yet the early Church Fathers, numerous mystics throughout the centuries, New England transcendentalists, poets, novelists and contemporary psychologists definitely have done so. Plato spoke of the reality of the soul in ancient Greece and compared it to a chariot; Origen believed in the pre-existence of the soul and its need for many reincarnations before union with God is achieved. Gregory of Nyssa acknowledged not only the immortality of the soul, but the resurrection of the body as well, both phenomena to be present before God at the time of final judgment. Many Christian mystics in their lives and writings speak of the need for sacrifice, the willingness to suffer for others, as a prerequisite to *extensio animi ad magna*, "the stretching of the soul to great things." Poets such as John Keats and William Wordsworth consistently referred to the soul. A letter written by Keats in 1819 advises his friends, "Call the world if you please 'the vale of Soul-making' ''"; and Wordsworth, in his "Lines Composed a Few Miles Above Tintern Abbey," describes how "we are laid asleep in body, and become a living soul." Ralph Waldo Emerson believed in an "over-soul," a universal soul of which everything living is a part, and his spirituality was related to that concept. "The time is coming," he said at Harvard Divinity School in 1838, "when all men will see that the gift of God to the soul is not a vaunting, overpowering, excluding sanctity, but a sweet, natural goodness, a goodness like thine and mine, and that so invites thine and mine to be and to grow."

In this century, novelist E. M. Forster explicitly acknowledges the soul in his works, especially in the popular *A Room With a View*. Mr. Emerson confronts Lucy, the woman whose young adult life has been characterized by a great deal of self-delusion regarding her relationship with his son George:

> "You love George! . . . You love the boy body and soul, plainly directly, as he loves you, and no other word expresses it. . . . I know by experience that the poets are right: love is eternal. . . . I only wish poets would say this, too: love is of the body; not the body, but of the body. Ah! the misery that would be saved if we confessed that! Ah! for a little directness to liberate the soul! Your soul, dear Lucy! I hate the word now, because of all the cant with which superstition has wrapped it round. But we have souls. I cannot say how they came nor whither they go, but we have them, and I see you ruining yours. I cannot bear it. It is again the darkness creeping in; it is hell."

Lucy does not understand what he is telling her at first, but because of the older man's gentle mentoring of her, "as he spoke the darkness was withdrawn, veil after veil, and she saw to the bottom of her soul." She was then able to take the necessary steps from the hell that her illusions had created and toward a commitment of love which brought tremendous joy.

We are already aware that Jung equated the soul with the *anima*, the unconscious, our roots, our past. According to another psychologist, James Hillman, the soul lives in the "vales," the valleys, the world of the feminine. "The soul's way is the way of dreams, reflections, fantasies, paintings, myths, story-telling." The soul has, Hillman says, "other voices and intentions than the one of the ego," and we must learn to listen to them; "the soul has an inherent composite nature with many gods reflected in this composition. Soul-making does not deny the gods and the search for them; it is rather a going deeper into ground, earth, death, concrete realities, and animating all of them." Hillman also equates the soul with history—our individual history, our culture as history, our religious history. Any progress in therapy or healing "requires recognition of history, an archaeology of the soul, a digging in the ruins, a re-collecting."

The Spiritual Mentor as Midwife of the Soul

Spiritual mentors can help others discover their souls by first of all paying attention to the reality of their own souls and bringing them to birth. We can do this by learning more about our individual histories, by recognizing the myths of our heroes, by digging in the ruins of our spiritual traditions, which we too often have ignored as a Christian people, by listening to our dreams, by telling the story of our lives and by re-collecting all with the help of God. This, of course, presupposes respectful attentiveness to our own experiences of soul.

All of us, as we grow older and listen more closely to our bodies as well as our dreams, have the potential for discerning the soul's powerful presence. We can discover it not only when we feel mysteriously connected with certain friends or with people whom we have never met, but also when, as Hillman reminds us, we go deeper into the ground, earth, death, concrete realities and listen for its presence. If we visit a place or country for the first time, we may experience the reality of the soul when we have a deep, inner sense that we have already been there. We may experience soul in our times of grief, as Augustine did when he lost a friend and came to the realization that they shared "one soul in two bodies'' and that his friend's soul was the ''other half'' of his. We may have intimations of the soul associated with experiences of great joy and fulfillment at the accomplishment of some aspect of our Dream or in the recovery of some forgotten aspects of our childhood. We may discover the presence of soul in our ability to endure some unexpected crisis or transition when we feel especially vulnerable.

One of the first experiences of soul that I had, one in fact that awakened me to the soul's reality, was with the death of my Grandma Mary, my grandmother with Irish roots, who helped raise me when I was very young. Although her death had been expected and the grief anticipated in my family long before she died at the age of 91, I could not have consciously predicted my response to that loss. After her wake I deliberately sought a few moments alone at her coffin in order to tell her good-bye. Unexpectedly, tears came from deep within me that spoke to me not only of the experience of great loss, but of gratitude for a relationship of great friendship, much greater than I was consciously aware. It was then that I became conscious of how closely her soul was intertwined with mine; how much my conscious interests, passions and pursuits were rooted in the heritage I had received through her.

Since then I have reflected upon and attempted to name other experiences of soul. Many of them are not associated with grief but with great joy. On Jo Anne's and my honeymoon in Europe years ago I unexpectedly began to hum and sing songs from my childhood that I had long since forgotten. When we visited Ireland for the first time, I experienced as I walked in the monastic ruins of Glendalough, located in the Wicklow Mountains, a sense of having been there before, of coming home. I had the similar feelings when visiting Iona, off the coast of Scotland, where Columcille went into exile fleeing from his past and at Melrose in Scotland and Lindisfarne in England, where the Celtic monk Cuthbert lived and ministered as a spiritual guide.

In many instances I equate soul with sacred places, certain seasons and the presence of soul friends: springtime at Gethsemani Abbey in Kentucky when the numerous blossoms of trees and flowers are coming into bloom; Concord, Massachusetts, in the summer of the year when the breeze on Walden Pond gently rocks the waves; Oxford in the fall when the multicolored leaves, carried by the wind, begin their gentle descent to the earth; and winter in St. Paul, with my family huddled around the blazing fire of our hearth and the Christmas tree, neatly trimmed, nearby.

C. S. Lewis associated experiences of great joy with a sensation of enormous bliss—"as if from a depth not of years, but of centuries." I believe such experiences are also of soul—of an ancient soul that was his, and that is ours as well.

Along with Jung in this century, Jewish scholar Abraham Heschel wrote of the reality of the soul. He said that the concept of a transmigration of souls contains a profound religious truth. "For one to know oneself, one must seek to understand one's past, one's heritage, the religious tradition from which one emerges." And he went on to state that "the human soul is born with a past." I agree. We inherit from our ancestors gifts so often taken for granted— our names, the color of our eyes and the texture of our hair, the unfolding of varied abilities and interests in different subjects, the desire to express our happiness in dance, the determination not to give in when crisis interrupts our lives, the passion to seek new worlds or to touch distant lands, the gift of being inspired by a prayer. If all this is ours as an inheritance, then why should we not acknowledge that our own souls may contain portions of other people's souls, intimations of past lives or ancestral memories long buried in our depths?

Each of us contains within our fragile vessels of skin and bones and cells this inheritance of soul. We are links between the ages, containing past and present expectations, sacred memories and future promise. Only when we recognize that we are heirs can we truly be pioneers.

The Spiritual Mentor as Pioneer

Although mentoring has a long and rich history, in many ways being a mentor today, especially for a lay person becoming a spiritual mentor, is being a pioneer. We must often face, as did my grandparents, the loneliness of being the first in an unknown land or ministry, the hardships of raising a family or meeting other responsibilities, the sense of being occasionally lost or rudderless, perhaps because we are ahead of our times, or because our times and church are just catching up with an ancient and valued practice. Sometimes, like Abraham and Sarah, we need the courage to leave the security of certain places and relationships in order to follow our call when everyone else may want us to stay put. Being a pioneer can mean being without role models as we attempt to break down old patterns of behavior that were taken for granted by our parents and grandparents and preceding generations, such as once seemingly clear distinctions between masculine and feminine, between the responsibilities of husband and wife, between expectations of society and church and self. At times it means being misunderstood, perhaps when we do not accept our spiritual heritage uncritically, but dare to ask the questions "What should be kept?" and "What should be left behind?" It may mean being resented when we fail to accept the argument that because "we have never done that before," we should not do so now.

Being a pioneer, who is first of all an heir, means not being satisfied with the slowness of ecumenical progress or the times of outright stalemate. Ecumenism is based upon our mutual recognition of common roots, our thirst for genuine community that values and is not threatened by diversity, and most of all, on our making friendships of the soul with those who share a different ecclesiology or spiritual heritage. Ecumenical progress will only occur when we attempt, as Thomas Merton suggests, to make of our lives a spiritual unity nurtured by friendships that transcend denominational, cultural and historical differences:

> If I can unite in myself the thought and devotion of Eastern and Western Christendom, the Greek and Latin fathers, the Russian with the Spanish mystics, I can prepare in myself the reunion of divided Christians. From that secret and unspoken unity in myself can eventually come a visible and manifest unity of all Christians.

So often it is through the diversity of friends and spiritual mentors with whom we have already become intimate that we discover a unity, a community already there. Convinced of the reality of the communion of souls, and convinced that if the past is to be a living thing we must add our own unique contribution to the present and future, we can go on to work for the transformation of church and society. Our ministries can make a difference, and every one of us should try.

Being pioneers aware of the soul's reality, we need to do as Hillman advises: some digging in the ruins, some re-collecting of our pasts. We only learn from the past when we are knowledgeable and appreciative of it. Recalling our histories, both familial and ecclesial, is a way of celebrating our inheritance, claiming it as ours, and most important, adding to it. This celebration includes both prayer and storytelling, forms of *anamnesis*, the remembrance of saving deeds that put us in touch with the living presence of God and our continuity with the past.

The Prayer of Remembrance

One of the most powerful forms of prayer is that of remembering and identifying all those who have mentored us in a significant way. We do this in the same manner we remember and identify the figures in our dreams. Once they have been named, using our creative imagination, we can carry on a conversation with them—not all of them at once, of course, but one by one—as a way of getting to know them better and, in the process, knowing ourselves more. Whether they are living or dead; whether we have ever met them in the physical sense or not, they can act as spiritual mentors, teaching us much about ourselves. In a very real sense they already are a part of us, but it is only when we pay some attention to them that we begin to understand their significance in our lives. As Sr. Donald Corcoran, a spiritual writer and guide, once advised me: "I must tell you that I had very strong impression, right after talking to you, that your grandmother is very close to you, will help you much, and that you should pray to her." Our spending time with spiritual mentors, perhaps with a grandparent or a wisdom figure from our Judeo-Christian traditions, in quiet reflection and journaling can be a very meaningful form of prayer. These prayerful conversations with our mentors can teach us wisdom and can lead us to the fount of wisdom, God.

Chaim Potok in *The Book of Lights* tells the story of Gershon Loran, an intense rabbinical student, who studies the Kabbalah, the Jewish book of mysticism and visions. Upon completion of his studies he is ordained a rabbi and goes to Korea as a chaplain. There, in the midst of a heavy schedule of responsibilities and a culture so foreign to him, he builds a *succah*, a hut, in which he can meditate and pray. There he is visited, the reader learns, by two of his former teachers and mentors, Nathan Malkuson and Jakob Keter, who, although thousands of miles away, continue to guide him. Sometimes they come separately and offer quite basic advice such as, "Take care of yourself, Loran. You look thin." At other times, they come together and begin their conversation with comments on his succah:

> "It is a big succah, Loran. You had in mind the seminary succah when you drew up the plans? The camouflage effect is intriguing. I think we will study a little, and then leave. What do you say, Keter?"
>
> "A little Talmud cannot hurt."
>
> "Not nearly as much as a little Kabbalah."
>
> "What shall we study, Malkuson?"
>
> Gershon sat very still and in his vision studied Torah with his two teachers, his *ushpizin*, his guests in the silent interior of his succah on this cool Korean night.

What makes the reader wonder, when the teachers first visit Gershon, is how they could be there when they are in reality so far from Korea. As the novel progresses the reader begins to realize that when a person studies the mystical tradition of the Kabbalah, time and space are not ultimate realities in relationships of intimacy and depth.

So also for our own soul friends or spiritual mentors. Whether a dead relative or a friend, a wisdom figure from the past, or a mentor who lives across town, they can be with us in our prayers and in our *succahs*, *poustinias*, cells or rooms. They are with us in whatever places we find for solitude, because, in fact, they already live in our souls and hearts. This prayerful way of remembering can lead to more effective ministry as well. Like the desert father Antony, when we remember what we have received from our mentors, we can incorporate the gift of themselves into our personalities, life styles and ministries.

The Recollection and Telling of Our Stories

The second form of digging in the ruins and re-collecting our pasts has to do with storytelling. We need to tell our stories to each other by writing about or re-creating the story of our lives. We also need to become acquainted with the stories of our ancestors and first mentors, for only when we have learned from them can we enter into dialogue with the stories of God's People in the scriptures or with the "great souls" of our Judeo-Christian heritage. There is much we do not know about ourselves that only our families can teach us. We may have books to tell us of our heritage, but it is from the stories of our ancestors that we learn the most. Their stories about themselves, about our parents, about us as children, tell us who we are and from where we came. Those stories contain within them the beginnings of our own wisdom.

I've heard many stories—as a child in the kitchen on my grandparents' farm, as a teenager on a fishing trip with Grandpa John that I thought would never end, at family gatherings celebrating baptisms, weddings and funerals. How my great-great-grandfather went to Wisconsin one winter rather than see his own son face the hardships of logging; how my grandparents bought their first car and Grandma Mary, with seven children, drove it through the window of the only restaurant in Kensal; how one night my father almost dropped two pails of milk on the farm where my mother was raised when her brothers, always mischievous, fired a shotgun into the air as a joke; how I used to carry cats back from the barn by their tails. I have been told these things, and in faith I believe them; they have colored and changed my own perception of who I am and where I've come from and to what family I belong. I share a family's history that is different in many ways from that of other families', but because I have been given a heritage through those stories, I can appreciate other people's heritages much more. I can also be more sensitive toward the plight of those in our society and world who have been deprived of their heritage or taught to deny it because it supposedly has little worth or questionable value. We need to listen when stories are told, but we also need to become storytellers for our own children and those we mentor—putting them in touch with stories and values that they might eventually claim freely as their own.

With every generation we must begin all over again, teaching our children the realities of life and death, of eros and psyche, of heart and soul. The spiritual community is our most valuable heritage, as well as the greatest gift we can give our children and those whom we choose to mentor. It is the gift of seeing with the heart, of helping others perceive that there is more to life than what we see with our eyes or what our culture may have come to value. It is based on the conviction that death itself has no lasting endurance, for life is the greater power that unites us with those we love and who have loved us. Somehow every generation must discover this for itself, and yet there is a way we can prepare them for that discovery. The way is through developing a spirituality based on care and participating in ministries of mentoring.

When our ancestors and mentors die, a link with our origins and our identities is broken and Mystery takes over once again. Sometimes, paradoxically, it is their leaving us that leads us to recognize the sacredness of our own lives and the mystery that constantly surrounds us. As C. S. Lewis wrote after the unexpected death of his close friend Charles Williams: "When the idea of death and the idea of Williams met, it was the idea of death that changed." It is this recognition of mystery that can lead us to our search for God with the help of mentors and friends. They are the ones who have given us life and legacy, and so we give others that life and pass on to them our own legacy, never binding them to us, but giving them the freedom to discover and pass on theirs.

The task of every mentor and soul friend, as Jesus himself revealed to his group of friends in his own ministry of spiritual mentoring, is this: to share stories with those who come after us, to point them back to their family origins and spiritual heritage, to bless them on their sacred journeys through time.

Conclusion

Your friend is the companion of your soul, another self.
      Aelred of Rievaulx, *Spiritual Friendship*

We began with a description of spirituality and the assertion that mentoring, especially spiritual mentoring, can be an important resource for developing our awareness of the sacred. In that context I presented some personal examples of mentors who have made a difference in my life. Throughout, I have attempted to engage you, the reader, in a dialogue with your own experiences of mentoring and our rich Judeo-Christian traditions of spiritual wisdom. In doing so I have presupposed that mentoring is a form of love and care that all of us, especially when we enter mid-life, can and must do if we are to maintain our humanity. For those of us who call ourselves Christian all mentoring is a special responsibility based on the perception and gratitude that we have been mentored first.

By focusing on the ministry of spiritual mentoring I hoped to give greater clarity to this ancient Christian practice and to invite more people to consider it for themselves. It is not just for priests and members of religious communities, but for all of us who desire to enrich other people's lives as we enrich our own spirituality. It presupposes knowledge of and respect for our lives and our spiritual traditions; it is dependent upon a continuing discernment of our vocations, often aided by attention to our dreams; it is intimately related to our commitment to ongoing conversion or change of heart.

The ministry of being a spiritual mentor or soul friend consists primarily of a friendship relationship between equals who bring their maturity and wisdom to each other's quest for holiness and God. In that mutual expression of questions, insights and gifts, both partners are changed and a communion of souls is born. An important contemporary ministry, it often consists of many overlapping roles and thus cannot be easily defined. For some who already have certain gifts and seek more competence through theo-

151

logical and psychological training, this ministry may become a profession of spiritual guidance or direction. The ministry itself, however, should not be equated with only the elite for the elite. Without in any way wanting to denigrate the competence we can gain by participation in apprenticeship or training programs, I believe that spiritual mentoring is a daily occurrence, done by all sorts and all ages of people without theological degrees or ministry certificates. It is an ancient Christian practice in which people discover a companion on their sacred journeys, a soul friend who is revealed as another self.

Whether we choose to become a spiritual mentor in a professional way or as a form of ministry, like Alcoholics Anonymous' tradition of sponsors, which can include almost anyone, certain insights emerge from our reflection that can help guide us in our ministries.

First, presupposing that all ministry flows out of who we are, we need to recognize that mentoring begins with ourselves. Thomas Merton would advise beginning with our own times of contemplation, solitude and self-reflection. If we want to be effective in spiritual mentoring, and really, in any form of ministry, our first duty, Merton says, is to see to our interior life ''and take time for prayer and meditation, since we will never be able to give to others what we do not possess ourselves.'' Thus, the importance of prayers of remembrance, as I suggested, and storytelling that starts with our own.

Second, we need to name and claim those qualities that already are ours, as well as develop those that do not come easily. Some of those qualities are outlined by St. Basil in his ascetical works. According to Basil the spiritual guide or mentor should be conversant with scripture, recollected, free from avarice, tranquil, pleasing to God, a lover of the poor, forgiving, preferring God to all things. We touched upon other qualities in our discussion of the Irish soul friend: compassion, maintaining confidentiality, openness and the ability to discern the movements of the heart. Effective mentoring is especially rooted in a spirituality that acknowledges and in many ways celebrates our limitations, allowing God to be the perfect one and not ourselves.

Third, we need to care for ourselves if we are to have the energy and patience to care for others. For many of us workaholics in ministry this means, quite simply, learning to relax. The desert father Antony (or Anthony) gives us counsel here—in a story told by Benedicta Ward in *The Desert Christian*:

> It is said of Anthony that one day he was relaxing with the brothers outside the cell when a hunter came by and rebuked him. Anthony said, "Bend your bow and shoot an arrow," and he did so. "Bend it again and shoot another," and he did—again and again. The hunter said, "Father, if I keep my bow always stretched, it will break." "So it is with the monk," replied Anthony; "if we push ourselves beyond measure we will break; it is right for us from time to time to relax our efforts."

Fourth, we need to take seriously the advice of developmental psychologists and begin to integrate the polarities within us between young and old, destruction and creativity, male and female. This means that, like the first mentor in *The Odyssey*, who was often impersonated by a woman, male spiritual mentors must develop their feminine side, and women their masculine side. One of the best examples of such a man is found in the diaries of the young woman, Etty Hillesum, who died at Auschwitz. In *An Interrupted Life*, one of the great spiritual classics of modern times, she describes her mentor Julius Spier as someone who, like a midwife, "had attended at the birth of my soul." He was perceived by others as something of a "lady's man." Etty writes:

> He is a lady's man, true enough, but only in the sense that, like Rilke, there is something about him to which women immediately respond and open up. And that is because he has so strong a feminine streak that he can understand how women feel—women whose souls can find no home since men will not join them to theirs. But in men like him the "soul" of a woman is given welcome and shelter. In that sense he is a lady's man, yes!

Despite his death, this man, who taught Etty how to pray, continues to act as her teacher. She says, "He teaches me something new every day,'' and as a result of his mentoring, ''my life has become an uninterrupted dialogue with you O God.''

Fifth, we need to recognize that sometimes mentoring can also include a ministry of absence. Although we cannot always be available, our lives and examples can speak louder than words. Augustine, for example, tells us in the *Confessions* that he was not able to ask his mentor, Ambrose, ''the questions I wanted to ask in the way I wanted to ask them, because I was prevented from having an intimate conversation by crowds of people, all of whom had some business with him and to whose infirmities he was servant.'' Still, Augustine observed his reading and prayer habits, listened to his preaching and was affected consciously and unconsciously by Ambrose in his own conversion process.

A sixth insight that can help our ministry is to understand that silence and few words can also be an important aspect of mentoring. Constant conversation doesn't necessarily mean better mentoring, and overly frequent meetings with a spiritual mentor do not guarantee personal growth. They may, in fact, be signs of too much dependency and not enough of centering our lives in God. Again, a story from our desert tradition contains a lesson for us:

> A monk once came to Basil of Caesarea and said, ''Speak a word, Father;'' and Basil replied, ''Thou shalt love the Lord thy God with all thy heart;'' and the monk went away at once. Twenty years later he came back, and said, ''Father, I have struggled to keep your word; now speak another word to me;'' and he said, ''Thou shalt love thy neighbor as thyself;'' and the monk returned in obedience to his cell to keep that also.

Finally, if the relationship itself is to be transformed rather than terminated in bitterness and anger, we as mentors need to learn when and how to let go of our expectations of the other person, and to let go sometimes of our own fear of being left behind, or even of our jealousy of who she or he is becoming, seemingly without us.

C. S. Lewis once again provides his wisdom. In *Till We Have*

Faces, he tells the story of Orual, the queen of a mythical land, and her relationship with her sister, Psyche. Her words to the gods reflect the way mentors sometimes feel rejected and left behind by those they have mentored:

> Can it be that you really don't understand? Do you think we mortals will find you gods easier to bear if you're beautiful? . . . You'll leave us nothing: nothing that's worth our keeping or your taking. Those we love best—whoever's most worth loving—those are the very ones you'll pick out. I can see it happening, age after age, and growing worse and worse the more you reveal your beauty: the son turning his back on the mother and the bride on her groom, stolen away by this everlasting calling, calling, calling of the gods. Taken where we can't follow. . . .
>
> We want to be our own. I was my own and Psyche was mine and no one else had a right to her. Oh, you'll say you took her away into bliss and joy such as I could never have given her, and I ought to have been glad of it for her sake. Why? . . .
>
> Did you ever remember whose the girl was? She was mine. MINE. Do you know what that word means? Mine!

And then Orual hears what she has said; indeed, what she has felt for so many years: "There was silence all around me. And now for the first time I knew what I had been doing. . . . There was given to me a certainty that this, at last, was my real voice, . . . the complaint was the answer."

While Lewis' words can act as a powerful reminder of our need for letting go of those we mentor as well as those who mentor us; while they confront us with our need to continually center our lives in the care of a loving God, our Judeo-Christian traditions consistently tell us of the value of having mentors and being spiritual mentors to others.

There is truth to what the book of Ecclesiastes says, "better two than one by himself [or herself]" (Eccl 4:9), and to what Charles Williams, C. S. Lewis' friend, warns us: "No mind is so good that it does not need another mind to counter and equal it, and to save it from conceit and bigotry and folly.'' Aelred of Rievaulx also expresses the positive dimensions of spiritual kinship:

> What happiness, what security, what joy to have someone to whom you dare to speak on terms of equality to another self; one to whom you need have no fear to confess your failings; one to whom you can unblushingly make known what progress you have made in the spiritual life; one to whom you can entrust all the secrets of your heart.

Recommended Reading

Introduction

1. Allchin, A. M. *The Living Presence of the Past*. New York: Seabury, 1981.

2. Buechner, Frederick. *The Sacred Journey*. San Francisco: Harper & Row, 1982.

3. Jung, Carl. *Four Archetypes*. Princeton, NJ: Princeton University Press, 1973.

4. May, Rollo. *My Quest for Beauty*. San Francisco: Saybrook, 1985.

Chapter One

1. Athanasius. *The Life of Antony*. Translated by Robert Gregg. New York: Paulist, 1980.

2. Bellah, Robert, et al. *Habits of the Heart*. New York: Harper & Row, 1985.

3. Bly, Carol. *Letters From the Country*. New York: Penguin Books, 1981.

4. Chaucer, Geoffrey. *The Canterbury Tales*. Edited by F. N. Robinson. London: The Folio Society, 1986.

5. Conn, Joann Wolski. *Women's Spirituality: Resources for Christian Development*. New York: Paulist, 1986.

6. Erikson, Erik. *Identity: Youth and Crisis*. New York: Norton, 1968.

7. French, R. M. *The Way of a Pilgrim, and the Pilgrim Continues His Way*. New York: Seabury, 1965.

8. Hazelden Foundation. *The Twelve Steps of Alcoholics Anonymous*. New York: Harper & Row, 1987.

9. Jones, Cheslyn, et al., eds. *The Study of Spirituality*. New York: Oxford University Press, 1986.

157

10. Julian of Norwich. *Showings*. Translated by Edmund Colledge and James Walsh. New York: Paulist, 1978.

11. Jung, Carl. *Modern Man in Search of a Soul*. New York: A Harvest Book, 1933.

12. Kennedy, Robert F. *To Seek a Newer World*. Garden City, NY: Doubleday, 1967.

13. Lattimore, Richard, trans. *The Odyssey of Homer*. New York: Harper & Row, 1975.

14. Leckey, Dolores. *Practical Spirituality for Lay People*. Kansas City, MO: Sheed and Ward, 1987.

15. Levinson, Daniel, et al. *The Seasons of a Man's Life*. New York: Alfred A. Knopf, 1978.

16. Lindbergh, Anne Morrow. *Gift From the Sea*. New York: Vintage Books, 1978.

17. Phillips-Jones, Linda. *Mentors and Proteges*. New York: Arbor House, 1982.

18. Spencer, Anita. *Seasons: Women's Search for Self Through Life's Stages*. New York: Paulist, 1982.

19. Sugg, Joyce, ed. *A Packet of Letters*. Oxford: Clarendon Press, 1983.

20. Underhill, Evelyn. *The Spiritual Life*. New York: Harper & Row, n.d.

21. Vaillant, George. *Adaptation to Life*. Boston: Little, Brown, 1977.

22. Warner, Rex, trans. *The Confessions of St. Augustine*. New York: A Mentor Book, 1963.

23. Whitehead, James and Evelyn. *Christian Life Patterns*. Garden City, NY: Image Books, 1979.

Chapter Two

1. Carpenter, Humphrey. *The Inklings*. Boston: Houghton Mifflin, 1979.

2. Como, James T., ed. *C. S. Lewis at the Breakfast Table*. New York: Macmillan, 1979.

3. Dorsett, Lyle, and Mead, Marjorie Lamp, eds. *C.S. Lewis: Letters to Children*. New York: Macmillan, 1985.

4. Giff, Jocelyn, ed. *Light on C.S. Lewis*. London: Geoffrey Bles Ltd., 1965.

5. Green, Roger, and Walter Hooper. *C. S. Lewis: A Biography*. New York: Harcourt Brace Jovanovich, 1974.

6. Griffiths, Bede. *The Golden String*. Springfield, IL: Templegate, 1954.

7. Hooper, Walter, ed. *They Stand Together: The Letters of C. S. Lewis and Arthur Greeves*. New York: Macmillan, 1979.

8. _____ . *Through Joy and Beyond*. New York: Macmillan, 1982.

9. Jung, Carl. *The Spirit in Man, Art, and Literature*. Princeton, NJ: Princeton University Press, 1966.

10. Keefe, Carolyn, ed. *C. S. Lewis: Speaker and Teacher*. Grand Rapids, MI: Zondervan Publishing Co., 1971.

11. Kilby, Clyde S., ed. *C. S. Lewis: Letters to an American Lady*. Grand Rapids, MI: Eerdmans, 1967.

12. _____ , and Mead, Marjorie Lamp, eds. *Brothers and Friends: An Intimate Portrait of C. S. Lewis*. San Francisco: Harper & Row, 1982.

13. Lewis, C. S. *A Grief Observed*. New York: Seabury, 1961.

14. _____ . *Reflections on the Psalms*. New York: Harcourt Brace Jovanovich, 1958.

15. _____ . *Letters to Malcolm: Chiefly on Prayer*. New York: Harcourt Brace Jovanovich, 1963.

16. _____ . *Mere Christianity*. New York: Macmillan, 1952.

17. _____ . *Spirits in Bondage*. New York: Harcourt Brace Jovanovich, 1984.

18. _____ . *Surprised by Joy*. New York: Harcourt, Brace, & World, 1955.

19. _____. *The Four Loves*. New York: Harcourt Brace Jovanovich, 1960.

20. _____. *The Pilgrim's Regress*. Grand Rapids, MI: Eerdmans, 1933.

21. _____. *The Screwtape Letters*. New York: Macmillan, 1949.

22. _____. *The Weight of Glory and Other Addresses*. New York: Macmillan, 1949.

23. Lewis, Warren, ed. *Letters of C. S. Lewis*. New York: Harcourt Brace Jovanovich, 1966.

24. Sayer, George. *Jack: C. S. Lewis and His Times*. San Francisco: Harper & Row, 1988.

25. Vanauken, Sheldon. *A Severe Mercy*. New York: Bantam Books, 1979.

Chapter Three

1. Aelred of Rievaulx. *Spiritual Friendship*. Kalamazoo, MI: Cistercian Publications, 1974.

2. Chadwick, Nora. *The Celts*. New York: Penguin Books, 1970.

3. Colgrave, Bertram and R. Mynors, eds. *Bede's Ecclesiastical History of the English People*. Oxford: Oxford University Press, 1981.

4. de Paor, Maire and Liam. *Early Christian Ireland*. London: Thames & Hudson, 1978.

5. Hanson, R.P.C. *The Life and Writings of the Historical Saint Patrick*. New York: Seabury, 1983.

6. Hesse, Hermann. *The Glass Bead Game*. New York: A Bantam Book, 1969.

7. Hughes, Kathleen. *Early Christian Ireland*. Ithaca, NY: Cornell University Press, 1972.

8. _____, and Ann Hamlin. *Celtic Monasticism*. New York: Seabury, 1981.

9. Joyce, James. *Ulysses*. New York: Book-of-the-Month Club, 1982.

10. Kenney, James F. *The Sources for the Early History of Ireland: Ecclesiastical.* Dublin: Irish University Press, 1966.

11. Leclercq, Jean, Francois Vandenbroucke, and Louis Bouyer. *The Spirituality of the Middle Ages.* New York: Seabury, 1968.

12. Leech, Kenneth. *Soul Friend: The Practice of Christian Spirituality.* New York: Harper & Row, 1980.

13. Maher, Michael, ed. *Irish Spirituality.* Dublin: Veritas Publications, 1981.

14. McGuire, Brian Patrick. *Friendship and Community: The Monastic Experience, 350-1250.* Kalamazoo, MI: Cistercian Publications, 1988.

15. McNeill, John T. *A History of the Cure of Souls.* New York: Harper Torchbooks, 1965.

16. _____ . *Celtic Churches.* Chicago: Chicago University Press, 1974.

17. Murphy, Thomas, and Michael Rankin. "The Practice of Celtic Penance," in St. Meinrad School of Theology, *Resonance: Penance, the Ministry of Reconciliation.* St. Meinrad, IN: St. Meinrad School of Theology, 1966.

18. O'Faolain, Sean. *The Irish.* New York: Penguin Books, 1981.

19. Plummer, Charles. *Lives of Irish Saints,* vols. 1, 2. London: Oxford University Press, 1922.

20. Poschmann, Bernhard. *Penance and the Anointing of the Sick.* New York: Herder & Herder, 1971.

21. Ryan, John. *Irish Monasticism.* Dublin: Irish Academic Press, 1931.

22. Sands, Bobby. *One Day in My Life.* Dublin: The Mercier Press, 1983.

23. Watkins, Oscar D. *A History of Penance,* vols. 1, 2. London: Longmans, Green, and Co., 1920.

24. Wiesel, Elie. *Night.* New York: Avon Books, 1969.

Chapter Four

1. Armstrong, Christopher. *Evelyn Underhill*. Grand Rapids, MI: Eerdmans, 1975.

2. Baker, Russell. *Growing Up*. New York: Congdon & Weed, Inc., 1982.

3. Boisen, Anton. *Out of the Depths*. New York: Harper & Row, 1960.

4. Day, Dorothy. *The Long Loneliness*. New York: Harper & Row, 1952.

5. Griffiths, Bede. *The Golden String*. Springfield, IL: Templegate, 1980.

6. Haughton, Rosemary. *On Trying to Be Human*. Springfield, IL: Templegate, 1966.

7. _____. *The Liberated Heart*. New York: Seabury, 1974.

8. _____. *The Passionate God*. New York: Paulist, 1981.

9. _____. *The Re-Creation of Eve*. Springfield, IL: Templegate, 1985.

10. _____. *The Theology of Experience*. New York: Newman, 1972.

11. _____. *The Transformation of Man*. New York: Paulist, 1967.

12. Heschel, Abraham. *Man Is Not Alone*. New York: Farrar, Straus, and Giroux, 1951.

13. Jones, Alan. *Exploring Spiritual Direction*. New York: Seabury, 1982.

14. Joyce, James. *A Portrait of the Artist as a Young Man*. New York: Viking Press, 1964.

15. McBrien, Richard P. *Ministry: A Theological, Pastoral Handbook*. San Francisco: Harper & Row, 1987.

16. Mallon, Thomas. *A Book of One's Own: People and Their Diaries*. New York: Ticknor & Fields, 1984.

17. Merton, Thomas. *The Seven Storey Mountain.* New York: Harcourt Brace Jovanovich, 1976.

18. Niebuhr, Reinhold. *Leaves From the Notebook of a Tamed Cynic.* San Francisco: Harper & Row, 1980.

19. Newman, John Henry. *Apologia Pro Vita Sua.* Garden City, NY: Image Books, 1956.

20. O'Meara, Thomas. *Theology of Ministry.* New York: Paulist, 1983.

21. Rilke, Rainer Maria. *Letters to a Young Poet.* New York: W. W. Norton, 1934.

22. Sharrock, Roger, ed. *John Bunyan's The Pilgrim's Progress.* Baltimore, MD: Penguin Books, 1974.

23. Washington, James M., ed. *A Testament of Hope: The Essential Writings of Martin Luther King, Jr.* San Francisco: Harper & Row, 1986.

24. Whitehead, James and Evelyn. *Seasons of Strength.* Garden City, NY: Doubleday, 1984.

25. _____ . *The Emerging Laity.* Garden City, NY: Doubleday, 1986.

Chapter Five

1. Beevers, John, trans. *The Autobiography of St. Therese of Lisieux: The Story of a Soul.* Garden City, NY: Image Books, 1957.

2. Eliade, Mircea. *Shamanism: Archaic Techniques of Ecstasy.* Princeton, NJ: Princeton University Press, 1964.

3. Green, Julien. *God's Fool: The Life and Times of Francis of Assisi.* San Francisco: Harper & Row, 1983.

4. Griffin, John Howard. *A Hidden Wholeness: The Visual World of Thomas Merton.* Boston: Houghton Mifflin, 1979.

5. Guggenbuhl-Craig, Adolf. *Power in the Helping Professions.* New York: Spring Publications, 1971.

6. Julian of Norwich. *Showings.* New York: Paulist, 1978.

7. Jung, Carl, ed. *Man and His Symbols.* Garden City, NY: Doubleday, 1964.

8. _____. *Memories, Dreams, Reflections.* New York: Vintage Books, 1963.

9. _____. *Modern Man in Search of a Soul.* New York: Harvest Books, 1933.

10. _____. *Psychology and Religion: West and East.* Princeton, NJ: Princeton University Press, 1973.

11. _____. *The Archetypes and the Collective Unconscious.* Princeton, NJ: Princeton University Press, 1969.

12. _____. *The Practice of Psychotherapy.* Princeton, NJ: Princeton University Press, 1966.

13. Jung, Emma. *Animus and Anima.* Dallas, TX: Spring Publications, 1957.

14. Merton, Thomas. *Conjectures of a Guilty Bystander.* Garden City, NY: Image Books, 1968.

15. Moore, Robert, ed. *Carl Jung and Christian Spirituality.* New York: Paulist, 1988.

16. O'Faolain, Sean. *Vive Moi!* Boston: Little, Brown, and Co., 1963.

17. Potok, Chaim. *The Chosen.* Greenwich, CT: A Fawcett Crest Book, 1967.

18. Sanford, John. *Dreams: God's Forgotten Language.* Philadelphia: J. B. Lippincott Co., 1968.

19. Teresa of Avila. *The Interior Castle.* New York: Paulist,1979.

20. Tooker, Elisabeth, ed. *Native North American Spirituality of the Eastern Woodlands.* New York: Paulist, 1979.

21. Veilleux, Armand, trans. *The Life of Saint Pachomius and His Disciples, vol. 1.* Kalamazoo, MI: Cistercian Publications, 1980.

22. Waddell, Helen. *The Desert Fathers.* Ann Arbor, MI: University of Michigan Press, 1972.

Chapter Six

1. Atkinson, Brooks, ed. *The Selected Writings of Ralph Waldo Emerson.* New York: The Modern Library, 1940.

2. Baker, Carlos, ed. *Keats: Poems and Selected Letters.* New York: Charles Scribner's Sons, 1962.

3. Bremmer, Jan. *The Early Greek Concept of the Soul.* Princeton, NJ: Princeton University Press, 1983.

4. Campbell, Joseph, and Bill Moyers. *The Power of Myth.* New York: Doubleday, 1988.

5. Cavarnos, John. *St. Gregory of Nyssa on the Origin and Destiny of the Soul.* Belmont, MA: Institute for Byzantine and Modern Greek Studies, 1982.

6. Forster, E. M. *Howard's End and A Room With a View.* New York: Signet Classic, 1986.

7. Griffin, Emilie. *Clinging: The Experience of Prayer.* San Francisco: Harper & Row, 1984.

8. Hartman, Geoffrey, ed. *The Selected Poetry and Prose of Wordsworth.* New York: A Meridian Book, 1970.

9. Heschel, Abraham. *Who Is Man?* Stanford, CA: Stanford University Press, 1968.

10. Hillman, James. *Archetypal Psychology: A Brief Account.* Dallas, TX: Spring Publications, 1985.

11. _____. "Peaks and Vales." In *On the Way to Self-Knowledge.* Ed. Jacob Needleman and Dennis Lewis. New York: Alfred Knopf, 1976.

12. Jones, Alan. *Soul Making: the Desert Way of Spirituality.* San Francisco: Harper & Row, 1985.

13. Lewis, C. S., ed. *Essays Presented to Charles Williams.* Grand Rapids, MI: Eerdmans, 1966.

14. Merton, Thomas. *Conjectures of a Guilty Bystander.* Garden City, NY: Image Books, 1968.

15. Potok, Chaim. *The Book of Lights.* New York: Fawcett Crest, 1981.

16. Russell, Norman, trans. *The Lives of the Desert Fathers.* Kalamazoo, MI: Cistercian Publications, 1981.

17. Sherwin, Byron. "Journey of a Soul: Abraham Joshua Heschel's Quest for Self-Understanding." *Religion in Life* (Autumn 1976).

18. Tillich, Paul. *The New Being.* New York: Charles Scribner's Sons, 1955.

Conclusion

1. Aelred of Rievaulx. *Spiritual Friendship.* Kalamazoo, MI: Cistercian Publications, 1974.

2. Hillesum, Etty. *An Interrupted Life.* New York: Pantheon Books, 1983.

3. Lewis, C.S. *Till We Have Faces.* Grand Rapids, MI: Eerdmans, 1956.

4. Merton, Thomas. *Spiritual Direction and Meditation.* Collegeville, MN: Liturgical Press, 1960.

5. Wagner, Sr. Monica, CSC, trans. *Saint Basil: Ascetical Works.* New York: Fathers of the Church, Inc., 1950.

6. Ward, Benedicta. *The Desert Christian.* New York: Macmillan, 1980.